Sunshine and Ice
Volume Z

LAYERS OF PERCEPTION

Martin Money

Published by New Generation Publishing in 2016

Copyright © Martin Money 2016

First Edition

The author asserts the moral right under the Copyright, Designs and Patents Act 1988 to be identified as the author of this work.

All Rights reserved. No part of this publication may be reproduced, stored in a retrieval system or transmitted, in any form or by any means without the prior consent of the author, nor be otherwise circulated in any form of binding or cover other than that which it is published and without a similar condition being imposed on the subsequent purchaser.

www.newgeneration-publishing.com

LAYERS OF PERCEPTION

Part One

May to September 2016

INTRODUCTION

Fractured Reality

Imagine, if you will, a species of malevolent inter-dimensional beings able to slip through cracks in the walls separating alternative realities and slide in and out of our five-sense world.

These cold-blooded entities, totally lacking normal human empathy and the mutual respect and compassion that go with it, are capable of possessing the bodies of people in power in order to force through an agenda of self-obsession, pure hatred and ruthless exploitation.

They may be reptilian or lizard, alien or other worldly – who knows? But they're Hell bent on world domination, using the rest of us as slaves, nothing more than brainwashed, unthinking flesh and blood robots serving them, their over-inflated egos and twisted ambitions.

Sounds like the plot of a science fiction movie. But there are those who claim that this is the stark truth, portrayed by Hollywood and TV as pure fantasy in a bid to throw us off the scent.

Oh, and they assert that showbiz, the music industry, the media, business, politics, religion and the military are all ultimately owned and controlled by these beings, working through those at the top in all these fields.

Their deeply negative energies are accessed and strengthened behind closed doors in the potent rituals of secret societies, it's alleged.

Me, I dunno, but it seems there's a fast-growing global movement of individuals who think these apparently crazy notions are the truth. They're certainly no madder than the warped, inconsistent and seriously fractured reality we're constantly asked to accept.

It's said these unfeeling entities operate outside our usual frequency band but can enter and leave it at will, dragging it down to a lower, darker, denser and more negative level.

Holy men, mystics and the more positively enlightened are in a constant battle with the hostile forces as they attempt to raise the frequency level for the benefit of the rest of us.

And the two energy streams – positive and negative – fight with each other inside of us all, coaxing us to do good and bad things, help or hurt each other. Religions externalize these impulses, labelling them God and Satan with vivid picture language to make the point.

Love and hate, light and dark, plus and minus. The eternal, animated dance of opposites.

For my part, I persevere in my search for truth, wisdom and enlightenment and continue to try and spread love, peace and harmony, bolstering the positive vibration/energy/frequency.

Here's the latest instalment of my decidedly weird but I hope entertaining and thought-provoking life journal. Fingers crossed, eh?...

****

CHAPTER ONE

Wistful Memories

May 17, evening – It would have been Jan's birthday today. I desperately miss my kind, thoughtful, generous, supportive, protective, loyal, loving, sweet big sister – the very epitome of the term.

I lit a candle for her earlier and put a little tribute on Facebook. A bit later, I went to the Bell because I needed to be with friends on such a traumatic day.

There, I saw Nicola Williams, Mark Evans, Laura Williams, Jem Hannen, Nicola's feller Mark Chastney, the pub dog Flick and others. It was cool – just what the doctor ordered.

May 18 – So the Premier League season has finished and Bournemouth have stayed up, finishing 16th out of the 20 teams (18th to 20th are relegated).

Newcastle, Norwich and Aston Villa go down while Burnley, Middlesbrough and one other team come up from the Championship – and that's between Hull and Sheffield Wednesday, who meet in the play-offs final later this month.

So it's many congratulations to manager Eddie Howe and the lads for surviving the club's very first season in the top flight. Onwards and upwards – next season top half of the table and the year after, getting into Europe, eh?

Hey, we can all dream – and just look at Leicester, fighting relegation for most of last season and coming from nowhere to win the league this year. This should give hope and inspiration to all teams including AFC Bournemouth.

May 19 – I'm currently thoroughly enjoying a Kinks compilation album, featuring that band's excellent pop rock which perfectly fitted the upbeat and exciting 1960s.

Chief songwriter Ray Davies has often been cited as a typically English wordsmith, conjuring up images of our beloved country in the flower power era and the early 1970s.

And indeed Waterloo Sunset, Set Me Free, You Really Got Me, Days, Dedicated Follower of Fashion, All Day and All of the Night, Tired of Waiting for You, Autumn Almanac and so on are brilliant snapshots bringing back wistful memories of a long gone era.

But it wasn't all hand-clapping, foot-tapping fun – there was a darker side to it. For example, Lazing on a Sunny Afternoon's cynical lyrics include a line about the singer's girlfriend leaving him to go back to her parents "telling tales of drunkenness and cruelty."

And Lola is a taboo-busting, groundbreaking little ditty about a transvestite – a brave departure in those still largely conservative, restrictive times.

Davies ranks alongside John Lennon and Pete Townsend as a skilled songwriter blending beauty with bitterness while keeping his finger firmly on the pulse of a fast-changing society.

Speaking of Lennon, I listened to Working Class Hero yesterday – an excellent 2005 compilation double album of all his best work, from his most beautiful (Woman, Oh My Love, Imagine, Love, Mind Games, Bless You) to most bitter (God, Working Class Hero, Gimme Some Truth, I'm Losing You, Cold Turkey).

I also played George Harrison's All Things Must Pass again – a classic and outstanding album that was the first one by an ex-Beatle to hit the top spot after they split.

May 22 – An EgyptAir plane carrying 56 passengers and 10 crew has crashed into the Mediterranean. Experts say flight data seems to suggest a bomb was detonated.

Closer to home, Manchester United yesterday won the 135th FA Cup Final, coming from behind to beat Crystal Palace 2-1 after extra time at Wembley Stadium.

Jason Puncheon broke the deadlock late in the second half and it briefly looked like being Palace's day until Juan Mata equalized just three minutes later.

United were then reduced to 10 men as Chris Smalling was red-carded for a second tasty tackle, making him only the fourth player in the tournament's history to be sent off.

But they held on until the 110th minute when Jesse Lingard launched a screamer that proved the winner.

The victory meant the club lifted the trophy for a record-equalling 12th time. The other team with that many wins is Arsenal.

But it's United's first silverware for three years and their general performance of late is seen as not good enough – especially their failure to qualify for the Champions' League next season by ending up fifth in the Premier League.

So within a day of their record-equalling achievement, manager Louis van Gaal has been ousted to make way for Jose Mourinho.

Portuguese legend Mourinho, highly successful with Chelsea, has been in United's sights and widely tipped to take over at Old Trafford since before Sir Alex Ferguson's retirement.

But I do feel sorry for Dutchman van Gaal, one of the most decorated managers in football.

Winning the FA Cup is no mean feat and he has notched up the impressive achievement of leading teams that lifted the comparable knockout trophies in three other countries too – Barcelona in Spain, Bayern Munich in Germany and Ajax in the Netherlands.

These teams also won their top flight leagues under him and as Dutch national coach he led that squad to a creditable third in the 2014 World Cup.

I've got the sublime Genesis on my CD player as I write – my sixth favourite band ever.

Turning to more weighty stuff, I seem to be watching more You Tube documentaries and music clips through my TV set than telly programmes at the moment.

It really is an eye-opener, finding fascinating and frequently outrageous material – a lot of which would never make mainstream media because of its reality-challenging content.

While intrigued, I certainly don't buy into it all. Most of it is thought-provoking, some of it mind-expanding but other parts alarmingly hate-laced or just plain weird. You Tube is saturated with the inane babblings of political and religious whack jobs.

I firmly believe in freedom of speech and expression and would adamantly defend these deranged oddballs' right to spout such nonsense. I'll continue watching with interest but please don't think for one minute I agree with every outlandish assertion. I don't.

But they do come in handy as I proceed with my search for truth, using gut instinct as my guide to sort the wheat from the chaff. And in this respect I've learned a great deal, making me wiser, more aware and more enlightened. Well I hope so anyway.

May 23 – Had a lovely time last night at the Bell with Nicola and Penny Williams, Dave Froud, Matt Brant, Mikey Delahaye, Demi Pitkin, Mark Chastney, John Gaynor, Ross Maslin, guv'nors Laura and Mark and others. Surweet!

Just playing a bit of Echo and the Bunnymen, just so you know. Cool!

May 24 – It would have been my 30th wedding anniversary today – had the marriage lasted more than seven years!

Oh well, stuff happens I suppose. Joe and I are okay, have been for yonks and have always got on. We went through a lot together – notably the whole heartbreaking baby John tragedy – and she then gave me my precious Phil, who in turn has given us our darling grandchildren.

We loved each other very much and were both head over heels but the cruel, upsetting, enraging world intervened to mess it all up. And I was a bit of a knob, if the truth be told.

But having our two boys forged an unbreakable bond between us that is there forever. I wish her all the happiness in the world – as I know she does me too.

Times like this you can't help asking yourself what if? Things could have turned out so differently had the marriage lasted and John lived – Just saying.

But would I swap the life I've had since? The bad bits yes, but there have been loads of good times – and laughs – thanks to my amazing family and friends.

I was crushed when the marriage collapsed because it was the last thing I wanted at the time. But I later came to realize that in many ways it liberated me to forge wonderful memories with great people that wouldn't have happened if Joe and I had stayed together.

All in all, I've done okay. More than okay actually.

I've got the brilliant Boston coming through my stereo speakers as I write. Led by guitarist, keyboard player, songwriter and producer Tom Scholz, the group – named after the city they came from – are a regular feature on rock radio stations the world over.

The CD I'm listening to is a compilation of all their classics – More Than A Feeling, Smoking, Amanda, Rock and Roll Band, Foreplay/Long Time, Don't Look Back, Tell Me, A Man I'll Never Be, Cool the Engines, Higher Power, Peace of Mind and so on. Superb!

It's my friend and close neighbour Billy Clarkson's birthday today so I wish him all the best.

May 25 – I popped to the Bell for a few beers yesterday afternoon. It was good to chat to Mark, Laura, Nicola, her feller Mark, Demi and a guy called Alex.

Today sees two more birthdays in my little corner of the world. One is that of Sarah Spence, a new friend I've recently made at the pub. She's the wife of British karaoke champion Darren Spence, another Bell regular who I've referred to in a previous book.

The other birthday girl is Isabella, Alison and Terry's second daughter, who is one year old. (Ali is my son Phil's step-sister.)

May 28 – Kicked off the Bank Holiday weekend in style yesterday (Friday) with a good booze and laughs session round my mate Sam Excell's with her and partner Carl Young, their sons Rudy and Bailey, Sam's daughter Becca, pet dogs Albert and Bramble and family friends Tina Mcauley, Jem Hannen, Rich Jeffery, Ryan Millen and Joedie Watt.

The only sour note was worrying news about Sam's state of health – doctors have referred her for urgent tests, suspecting her problems are symptoms of one or more serious conditions. We're all in her corner, hoping for the best.

Footballer Marcus Rashford made history yesterday as the youngest player to score on his debut for England.

Manchester United's Rashford, aged 18 years and 208 days, beat the previous record set by Tommy Lawton way back in 1938 as he volleyed in after only 138 seconds.

Wayne Rooney also scored as England beat Australia 2-1 in a pre-Euros friendly at the Stadium of Light, Sunderland.

I've been playing James Brown, the Isley Brothers, Iggy Pop and Chris de Burgh on my CD system. Chris de Burgh? – Well, yes, forget the bloody awful Lady in Red, he's actually a fine singer songwriter specialising in slow ballads and upbeat soft rock with witty lyrics.

Thought for the day: Control a man's property and you control his life, control his dreams and you control his soul.

May 29 – Went to Verwood yesterday for Isabella's first birthday party, which meant I saw my grandchildren Chloe and Harvey, my son Phil and his wife Emily and other family members. Very pleasant it was too.

May 30 – It's Bank Holiday Monday today and I'm having a quiet one, having gone a bit mad yesterday. I went to the Bell for three pints early afternoon and returned there during the evening to have a few more drinks, ending up at Nicola and Mark's till the early hours.

It was a very good session with them, Nicola's mum Penny, Jem Hannen, Mark Hemington, Tamzin Lee, Mikey Delahaye, Dave Froud and others. Fabulous!

June 1 – Had another fine afternoon up the Bell yesterday with Laura and Mark, Nicola, Laura's parents Steve and Mandy, another guy called Steve, pub puppy Flick and Jack, Mandy and Steve's terrier dog.

More sad news in the comedy world – telly sitcom writer Carla Lane has died aged 87. Liverpudlian Carla penned the family-based classics Bread and Butterflies and co-wrote the brilliant show The Liver Birds. She was also a passionate animal rights campaigner.

Today is Ronnie Wood's 69th birthday – you know, he of the Rolling Stones, previously in the Faces with Rod Stewart. Salutations Ron, thanks for the music, keep on rocking, son!

June 2 – Been relishing a superb Jeff Beck CD called Truth, featuring Rod Stewart, Ronnie Wood, Keith Moon, Jimmy Page, John Paul Jones, Madeline Bell, Nicky Hopkins and Aynsley Dunbar. Also listened to a bit of Faces and, to mix it up a bit, Bon Jovi.

Plus a Bob Dylan compilation double disc set and Led Zeppelin Two, my tenth favourite album of all time. I'm now playing a collection of live Stones tracks. Succulent sounds!

June 3 – The Stones are one of those bands who have eagerly embraced satanic references as part of their rebel stance and stagecraft. Black Sabbath too, and quite a few other groups and solo stars – especially in the heavy metal genre.

Provocative lyrics, costumes and artwork have all been part of what I perceive to be playful attempts to entertain using vivid imagery, mischief and an alluring hint of danger to intensify the experience, adding to its enjoyment.

It's all done in a similar vein to the frequent use of hand signals such as the "devil's horns" popular with rock audiences as well as politicians and popes.

In the case of "straight" conventional leaders these could indeed be blatant gestures showing allegiance to a particular global community agenda, often called the New World Order.

And those financing and controlling the music business might be serving that agenda in the same way as their counterparts in Hollywood, the media, politics, commerce, religion and the military.

But when it comes to the musicians themselves, I prefer to think of it in terms of tantalizing tongue-in-cheek fun not to be taken too seriously.

Unfortunately, some You Tube contributors do just that – and especially the more unhinged religious crazies.

And they go even further, repeating the hoary old chestnut about hidden demonic messages that can only be heard if you play the music backwards. Led Zeppelin and the Beatles are two of the most often quoted bands in this context.

But I'd suggest that the claims are overwhelmingly pure nonsense, really stretching a point, and any apparent references to Satan are decidedly flimsy and most likely accidental.

In the rare instances that they are deliberate, I'd maintain that again it's in a spirit of fun. The Beatles were so amused by people constantly reading far too much into their song words that they started including all sorts of intriguing messages – just to play along and take the piss.

There have even been decidedly implausible claims that the classic hippy peace hand sign is actually an alternative "devil's horns" gesture. Try telling that to Ringo! (He uses it a lot.)

Maybe my passion for rock and roll has given me a blind spot when it comes to allegations of demonic forces working through the artists I love. After all, I do accept it's possible in other areas of society where I have less empathy, such as politics, big business and the military.

But in all honesty I can't see John Lennon, Robert Plant, David Bowie, Pete Townsend or Bob Marley as willing servants of an evil, twisted agenda bent on ruthless world control. Their lyrics and interviews strongly suggest the complete opposite.

All these men – and many other people in showbiz – have consistently shown themselves to be free-thinking, independent-minded and wise individuals promoting positive messages.

It's true that Led Zep's Jimmy Page once lived in black magician Aleister Crowley's old home, a manor house near Loch Ness, Scotland. So what! – It doesn't make Page a Satanist. It simply signifies that he was intrigued by the occult in general and Crowley in particular.

The guitarist is quoted as saying he thought the building and its setting would provide an atmosphere very conducive to song writing.

Meanwhile, Black Sabbath, Alice Cooper, AC/DC and others have forged careers using the dark side as thrilling entertainment.

Song words have often reflected contemporary music's decades-old flirtation with provocative religious images such as angels, devils, Heaven and Hell.

They've even shown up in my own lyrics a fair old bit. Consider this:

"Is this the Devil's music? Well, book my ticket, Hell's my place" **(Terminal Case).**

An over-zealous You Tube theorist reading those words would declare "Ah ha! – There you have it, indisputable proof that he's openly admitting his allegiance to Satan."

Er, no. At the time I wrote that, I was simply attempting to compose a pretty standard rock lyric using potent, typical and familiar terminology. That's all.

I was certainly not advocating Devil worship or the black arts in any way, shape or form. And to suggest that I was would be just plain ludicrous – as mad as making such claims against the Stones, Sabbath, Alice, Led Zeppelin or the Beatles.

Or indeed Madonna, Katy Perry or any other music stars employing such vivid imagery.

I find rock, reggae and the rest so uplifting, life-affirming, often thought-provoking, highly enjoyable, frequently deeply spiritual and overwhelmingly positive. Music is good for us – and it would take a lot to persuade me otherwise.

And the best performers are the ones who write, play and sing from the heart. I'd rather listen to something that causes my soul to soar, raises my spirits, moves my body and makes me smile, cry and think than a sell-out fake rebel trying to flog me Coca Cola or fashion wear.

Or some safe as houses, bland and boring, talentless bunch of unthreatening pretty boys clogging the airwaves with mundane music for morons.

It's called integrity, folks – something that sadly far too many modern day pop stars don't seem to have.

June 4 – Boxing legend Muhammad Ali has passed away, aged 74.

He died in hospital after being admitted two days ago with a respiratory problem complicated by the Parkinson's disease he'd had for over 30 years.

The three times world heavyweight champion came to prominence in 1960 when he won an Olympic gold medal while still using his birth name of Cassius Clay. He later declared himself Muhammad Ali as a reflection of his Muslim faith.

He was an amazing boxer – arguably the best ever – but he will be remembered for far more than that.

His catchphrase was "I am the greatest" but the outrageous arrogance of his egocentric public persona is said to have masked a thoughtful, kind and generous spirit. He was, apparently, a true man of the people.

Born in Kentucky at a time when segregation was still very much alive and kicking and prejudice was commonplace, he became a passionate civil rights campaigner and a global spokesman for black citizens.

Frequently courting controversy, he was stripped of his world heavyweight title, very nearly went to prison and was banned from boxing for three years in 1967 when he refused to serve in the American military, citing his Islamic beliefs and opposition to the Vietnam War.

He was a man of principles. But he's as famous for his wit, wisdom and clever wordplay as his boxing skills or campaigning. He was shrewd, had integrity and appealed to millions who didn't even like boxing, me included.

BBC TV viewers once voted him sports personality of the 20th century. But his huge legacy transcended sport and he was one of the most recognized men on the planet. He was a true icon in every sense of the word. RIP champ – thanks for entertaining and inspiring us.

Yesterday being a Friday, I strolled up to Sam and Carl's for our usual weekly booze and silliness catch-up session – and left with blue hair! Oh well, at least it covers up the grey.

Apart from the couple and their two little boys – Rudy and Bailey – Sam's daughter Bec was present with her feller Cameron, family pet dogs Albert and Bramble, Christina Mcauley, Jem Hannen and Rich Jeffery.

June 5 – It's Sunday morning and I'm listening to the wonderful Sergeant Pepper album by the Beatles. Just played it once but I'm going to enjoy the entire ear pleasing, heart-lifting experience all over again immediately because it's so damned good.

I've chosen to revisit the sonic delights of this masterpiece in honour of the fact it was released 49 years ago this weekend. It hit the top of the charts and notched up a total of 27 weeks there, 23 of them consecutive. Ah, those were the days!

This brilliant, groundbreaking, truly iconic long player changed music forever. It's been widely hailed as the greatest of all time. But much as I admire, adore and treasure it, it's not my number one. I don't even think it's the best Beatles album.

Anyone who knows me or has read my books will appreciate how much I love this band – for their musical genius, humour, wit, wisdom, warm personalities and spot-on attitudes. They're my all time favourite group and a major influence and inspiration on my life.

Readers of *Persistent Illusions* will have learned that in fact, Pink Floyd's Dark Side of the Moon is my top album ever, with Revolver at number two and Sergeant Pepper third.

I fully endorse everything that's been said about Pepper's importance and standing as a cultural landmark but I just happen to think that – by a very slim margin – song for song, Revolver is more inventive, varied and ultimately stronger.

And it was more of a group effort – it had three George Harrison compositions on it, all of them better than the admittedly very good Within You Without You, the only song of his on Sergeant P.

Speaking of people I love, I watched some old recordings of Bill Hicks shows on You Tube last night – there being the usual Saturday evening pathetic, mind-numbing dross on the telly.

I've referred to this exceptional man before. For anyone who doesn't know, he was an American stand-up comedian who tragically died far too soon in 1994 at the age of only 32.

He used his acerbic wit to provide a refreshingly different, brutally honest view of reality that continues to make a growing number of people think "yeah, that guy knew the score."

This wise, perceptive and very funny man was a pioneer visionary way ahead of his time. Most of us who now feel the same took a while to catch up and nod appreciatively while creasing up at his brilliant turn of phrase and potent comic delivery.

Sadly, far too many of the half-asleep herd still don't get it. But more and more are now waking up and declaring: "Damn – he nailed it." Not only him – others too.

His frank statements – about smoking, alcohol, drugs, religion, politics, the shopping mall society, war and the callous elite running things and controlling us – frequently got him into trouble, especially in the USA. He was better appreciated in England, becoming a cult hero.

His beliefs and philosophy closely reflect my own and I've quoted him in previous books so I won't do it again. Like the Beatles, he's an inspiration to me. Catch film footage of his concerts and interviews – if you're on the same wavelength, you'll get it and love him too.

When it comes to the reality war, I'm very much on the side of Bill Hicks, Russell Brand and David Icke. There are frequent and intriguing overlaps in what these three – and many others – have said and stand for.

Because make no mistake, it is a war – an intensifying war of ideas between those that accept the status quo, either enthusiastically promoting or tacitly supporting it, or detest and oppose it with a blazing passion for things to change for the better. Like me.

I'm very much on the side of the quiet revolution, passive resistance and peaceful non-cooperation brigade. Gandhi had the right idea.

Hard-hearted politicians, cruel selfish control freaks and dull materialists can sod off. I'm with Gandhi, Carl Jung, Albert Einstein, William Blake, Lewis Carroll, Martin Luther King, Bill Hicks, Russell Brand, David Icke, Bob Marley and John Lennon – every flipping time.

And I say thank goodness for the Dalai Lama, the Monty Python team, Dan Brown, John Sullivan, the Matrix movie makers, Richard Curtis, Russell Howard, Seth MacFarlane and others spreading love, hope, humour, joy, insight and wisdom.

We desperately need such people to counteract an apparently deeply depressing reality where the media seems totally obsessed with bad news, negative stereotypes and creating conflict.

****

CHAPTER TWO

Sipping Pints In The Sun

June 6 – Yesterday evening up the Bell was another cracking session in the pub I've fallen in love with all over again. Loads of familiar faces were there including my new friends Krissie Benbow and Alex King, who were both celebrating their birthdays.

Mark and Laura were joined by Matt Brant, Jenny Daniels, Ben Avill, John Gaynor, Mark "Tich" Hemington, Penny and Nicola Williams, Nicola's man Mark, Jem Hannen, Gary Preston, Ollie Okoye, Mikey Delahaye, his mum Lou, her feller Brian, Demi Pitkin, Lottie Wragg, Simon "Squeak" Turnbull, his lady Ruth, Darren, Harry Evans, DJ Ross and others.

It was excellent, really cool. My local drinking hole is now back to how it was before those grim wilderness years that in truth started quite a while ago as a lot of the old crowd drifted away during the tail end of Lou and Trudy Brencher's reign as guv'nors.

It just seemed to get a lot worse in the five years under their replacement managers when the pub was relaunched as Seabourne's Bar, a ridiculous moniker that I and many others hated.

Laura and Mark's decision to revert to its original name was a shrewd and popular master stroke as they proceeded to revive it as a proper local pub again – with dogs and children and a real family, community air – rather than just a building where people drank.

Now here's a very interesting news item – Swiss voters have overwhelmingly rejected a plan to introduce a basic income for all regardless of work.

Almost 77 per cent opposed the idea with only 23 supporting it.

It had been proposed that all adults be paid a guaranteed monthly income of 2,500 Swiss francs (£1,755) whether or not they have jobs.

The yes camp argued that as work was increasingly automated, available jobs were getting scarcer and scarcer. But Swiss unemployment remains relatively low.

What interests me is that this has actually been put forward and considered by a nation. I've previously promoted such a scheme for us but wondered if it was actually practical.

Switzerland, not in the European Union, instead has a fair old number of separate trade treaties by which half its exports go to EU countries and it has lucrative deals with other territories as well including China. Plus it has no immigration problem.

It also has a democratic system said to be far more worthy of the description and one of the highest standards of living in the world. It has stayed fiercely neutral when others have fought wars and is often held up as a model country for others to emulate.

With that all-important "stay in or leave the EU" referendum just around the corner in the UK, those advocating we pull out are pointing to Switzerland as excellent proof that we don't need to be in it.

June 7, 7 pm – Just had a lovely afternoon at The Bell with Paula, birthday girl Krissie Benbow, her feller Paul Clyde, Laura and Mark, Nicola, her man Mark, her mum Penny, Alex, Matt, Lee, Ian, Darren, Aussie Stu, Brian, Lou and her son Mikey. Cool!

Before going to the pub, I had a bit of a heavy metal morning listening to Black Sabbath, Motorhead and Saxon. Before that I did my exercises and played my bass and six-stringed guitars for a while.

I've just had a thought. If anyone has an issue with how I spend my time and who I spend it with, I'm afraid that's their problem, not mine. We can all mess up but we live and forgive – if mature, balanced and strong enough, that is – especially when it comes to those we love.

Having it otherwise is self-defeating folly.

June 8 – As usual, Paula and I had a good old chat, catch up and numerous laughs at our now customary four-weekly rendezvous at the pub yesterday.

As we sat in the beer garden, sipping pints in the sun, she asked me what I do with my days. I was surprised – I thought she knew.

But, thinking about it, it's probably a question most of my mates with jobs, partners, children and jam-packed, busy lives would also like answered, although I can't understand why. Without being rude, what difference does it make to them?

But they're my pals and Paula's one of my closest. So in her case I didn't mind providing her with a straight, honest reply.

I told her what I'd done that day before we met up in the early afternoon – got up, showered, dressed, had breakfast, took my medication, did my light exercises, played my guitars, had a cup of tea while listening to music, changed, had a sandwich then sauntered up to the Bell.

I go to the shops or for a walk most mornings and often write a bit of this ongoing *Sunshine and Ice* journal while listening to music, although yesterday I left it until I returned home from the pub. It's one of my major functions nowadays. It's what I do and what I am.

I check Facebook twice daily, have my main meal and a cuppa noon to 1pm and usually doze off afterwards while watching daytime TV. Early evenings I have a snack, read for an hour or so then either resume watching telly, put on DVD or find something on You Tube.

The days I drink alcohol during the afternoon or early evening I reverse my eating regime, having a light lunch beforehand and my main meal afterwards, sometimes a take-away.

I see my mates Sam and Carl on Fridays, go to the pub once or twice a week, meet up with Phil, Emily and the grandkids and other family members roughly monthly, occasionally attend gigs and I've also been on short, relatively cheap holidays once every year or two.

I regularly visit my very good buddy Jem, sometimes go other places, usually meet my sister Carol, hubby David and our "adopted sister" Suzette for a Christmas meal and hook up with my chum and former work colleague Lea annually for a festive drink and chinwag.

You know, the usual stuff other people do – although now the money's once again getting tight and I'm back on welfare, I'm pulling in my horns financially on all fronts.

And, of course, I live alone so have to keep my flat presentable and look after myself, cooking and so on. All that together pretty much takes up my time. Normal paid or unpaid work and a busier life are beyond me now – I can't take the stress and don't have the energy.

I remain young at heart but my body tells me otherwise. In this tenaciously persistent illusion of reality, tied inextricable to false notions of time, I'm 62 years old and past my best. So I've needed to slow down, especially in light of my cardiac situation.

Although I no longer accept the false paradigm we're constantly spoon-fed, I still need to use it to my own ends in order to survive, as we all do. That's the infuriating paradox for me.

So there you have it. The quiet life suits me fine and I certainly don't get bored. I've done my dashing about like mad – years of it. Now I leave it to others, and good luck to them.

I look forward immensely to seeing Sam and Carl, Paula, the family, my Bell friends and others. The fact that I don't go to the pub on a daily basis like I used to all those years ago, or see my friends and loved ones more frequently, only adds to the pleasure of it when I do.

And thanks to Laura, Mark, Nicola and my constantly-expanding circle of drinking pals, the pub is once again actually worth going to. At long last it's been restored as my beloved Bell.

As if to make a point, writing today's entry in this book has taken more than an hour. Earlier I went to a shop. Now it's getting on for lunchtime. That's another morning nearly gone.

The sounds of David Bowie are coming through my stereo speakers as I prepare to sign off, at least for the time being. I'll resume this junk-loaded journal when I once again feel inspired. Something tells me it won't be long!

June 9 – I was right! Here comes today's not-so-gripping instalment…

The fiercely battling "in" and "out" campaigns intensify daily as the big UK referendum over the European Union draws ever closer. We go to the polls a fortnight today.

As I've said before, we should have had this vote decades ago, we've become inextricably pulled into the web, it's far too late to exit now, it could be disastrous for our economy and all we can do at this stage is press our politicians to try and transform it from the inside.

The Green Party, of which I'm a lifelong member, supports staying in and working alongside other countries' Greens to make the EU more truly democratic and environment friendly.

I tend to agree – but the rebel in me wants to vote "leave", just to register my disgust at the way we're being led towards total submission to an iron-fist regime of centralized power.

So I'm currently wavering – and the bullshitters and scaremongers aren't helping at all.

Either way, we should retain our own independence and sovereignty while working closely with our neighbour countries and the wider world to promote peace and harmony and protect our species, our planet and its resources – for everyone's sake.

But one thing's for sure – the exit advocates are misleading us by suggesting it would be easy to extricate ourselves at this late stage. It wouldn't. It would be a monumental gamble. It might well pay off, leading to our country thriving again, but it could well spell trouble.

Chances are that the fear of dire consequences if we leave will secure a majority vote to stay. But even if it does go the other way, I've a strong feeling that events will then be manipulated to ensure that we end up thinking it was the wrong decision and so we should reverse it.

That is, after all, the game plan – and nothing gets in the way of the game plan, least of all the people. So I suspect the referendum could well be just another academic exercise, like the Parliamentary elections that ultimately have little influence on the way things are organized.

This is one reason I'm seriously thinking of switching from pragmatic "remain" to bold "leave" – as a protest vote, because we'll be staying in anyway, one way or the other.

God I'm cynical sometimes! But I'm fed up with the incessant lies, scare tactics and ruthless exploitation being passed off as political home truths.

I worry about our future myself but I'm not trying to frighten anyone – just pondering possible scenarios. It's time to get things into perspective. The sun will rise on a new day after the referendum whatever the outcome. The Earth will continue to spin on its axis.

And besides, I do genuinely share concerns that we're being told what to do by unelected Brussels bureaucrats when it comes to making our laws and controlling our borders.

Sure, some EU regulations are welcome, particularly those protecting people's rights, and immigrants have brought skills and customs benefitting our UK countries for centuries, but the sheer volume of them arriving now, being dictated by our EU overlords, is a huge worry.

Yes, we should ensure our growing population is adequately housed and money is ploughed into the NHS and other community services to keep pace with the demands for them.

I accept that immigrants give much more to Britain than they take from it. But a fast, unfettered flow of them could be a destabilizing influence bringing friction and problems.

Control of numbers, common sense and compassion are all desperately needed here to avert a growing crisis. Unfortunately, there seems to be a distinct lack of all three.

Today is the second anniversary of Rik Mayall's passing. I've lit a candle for the highly talented and very popular comedy star. Ye gods! – two years? Really? Time flies don't it?

I've been enjoying ZZ Top, the Tygers of Pan Tang, AC/DC and Metallica.

June 10 – I'm playing the live Pink Floyd album Pulse as I write. A bit earlier I once again revelled in Black Sabbath's excellent Heaven and Hell, one of my all time top 20 long players. It's certainly my favourite by that group.

Ozzy Osbourne fans would be horrified as he's not on it – Ronnie James Dio's the vocalist. But, much as I love Paranoid, Sabbath Bloody Sabbath, Black Sabbath Four, Master of Reality and the ground-breaking eponymous first album, there's something extra here.

It brims with enthusiasm and joy, every track's a winner, the band play so damned well and really tight and the production is superb. This is intelligent, crisp, invigorating hard rock at its very best. Sorry Ozzy, you're brilliant too but that's how I feel.

The Euro 2016 football tournament kicks off later today with host nation France taking on Romania in the opening match. England's first group game is against Russia tomorrow evening. Come on Roy's boys!

June 11 – France beat Romania 2-1 to set the standard and firmly establish themselves as the much-fancied home team that the visiting squads need to beat.

Let's have faith that England can spoil the party and walk away with the trophy. Don't laugh – why the Hell not? We won the World Cup once – in 1966 – and it's high time we clinched the Euro Cup for the first time ever. We need to believe – and the players especially. Go lads!

Had another good session round Sam and Carl's last night including consumption of Sam's own cocktail – Strawberry and melon flavour juice with vodka, lemonade and a touch of sugar. She named it the "jelly tot" as it tasted just like the kids' sweets of the same name.

June 12 – England drew 1-1 with Russia, a disappointing outcome bearing in mind that it looked as if we were going to pick up all three points until they scored a header in stoppage time with only two minutes or so left to play.

Our lads dominated possession, creating chance after chance, but frustratingly couldn't put any away until Tottenham's Eric Dier blasted in a 20-yard free kick with 17 minutes to go.

Some of Roy's boys excelled but others were decidedly under par. Full marks for energy, enthusiasm and persistence but not many for accuracy or results I'm afraid. We'll have to do a lot better than that if we're going to at least reach the semi-finals, as many have predicted.

Having said that, there were a lot of positives to build upon as the fellers prepare to face Wales in four days' time. They top our group after beating Slovakia 2-1 earlier yesterday.

Unfortunately, violence marred the closing stages of our game. Russian fans are said to have let off flares after their team equalized and then broken through a barrier to charge and attack fleeing England supporters. Scores of people were taken to hospital where one is critically ill.

The incident followed three days of running battles between rival fans in Marseilles, where the match took place. Let's just hope Euro 2016 is remembered for football, not fighting.

Just enjoying a bit of the Libertines – good, intelligent catchy pop rock with a 1960s feel to it.

June 13 – It's a terrible Monday morning in America. Fifty people were killed and 53 more wounded when a gunman went berserk at a nightclub in Orlando, Florida, in the early hours yesterday.

It's the worst peacetime mass shooting event in the country's history. The gunman, named as Omar Mateen from Afghanistan, was himself shot dead by police in the aftermath.

I see three possible explanations for this atrocity causing tragedy and trauma. The first is the official story – that he was a servant of the savage, violent, and widely hated Islamic State.

The second is that he was an unhinged homophobic – the night spot where it happened is a known hang out for gay people.

Both versions have been widely bandied about since the incident.

But there is a third scenario, not nearly so popular because it raises far too many uncomfortable and very inconvenient questions, especially for those in power.

Some so-called conspiracy theorists have already claimed that Mateen was no bigoted lone nutcase, nor was he a violent radical convert to Islamic extremism.

They suggest that he was in fact a brainwashed mind control slave being used by sinister forces within the American secret services to further discredit and demonize Muslims.

I must say that thought had crossed my mind as well. Similar claims have been made about Lee Harvey Oswald – the guy who shot John Kennedy – his brother Bobby Kennedy's killer Sirhan Sirhan and Mark Chapman, who gunned down John Lennon.

All three victims were high profile men with the passion, integrity and courage to challenge the deeply corrupt status quo.

As always, we will never be told the truth of any of these matters and are therefore destined to speculate for all eternity. The only thing we know for sure is that 50 more people are dead and over 50 more injured, and their families and friends will bear the emotional scars for life.

And that's both very sad and totally unacceptable to anyone with a heart and conscience.

In UK news, Prime Minister David Cameron is getting more desperate by the day as the exit Europe campaign appears to gain ground. His latest bid to scare us all silly centres on pensions and public finance. He says both are seriously under threat if we leave the EU.

Seems to me he's panicking like mad while setting us up for more deeply damaging budget cuts as he then smugly declares "I warned you" – using it as a cynical excuse rather than admitting that his brutal austerity measures hitting the disadvantaged hardest have failed.

Good grief! – With this uncaring, untrustworthy millionaire trying to scare us into voting remain and those ludicrous loons Boris Johnson and Nigel Farage demanding we choose to leave, it's no wonder so many people are still undecided on which way to go.

This is a crucial issue so give us the proper facts in a balanced way you odious cretins, not wildly over the top and alarming declarations based on lies and distortions!

In the Euro football competition, Germany beat Ukraine 2-0 but Northern Ireland – in their first major tournament for 30 years – went down 1-0 to Poland.

And tournament organisers UEFA have warned that they will consider expelling Russia and England's teams if there's any repeat of the violence that occurred before and at their match.

Well, I'd argue that the players shouldn't be penalized for the actions of a few violent morons and if anyone is to be expelled, it should follow a full inquiry into what happened and why.

Granted, TV news film footage appears to show that England fans were involved in fights and riots before the game – but I'd point out that just because an unhinged thug is wearing an England shirt or waving an England flag that doesn't make them a genuine supporter.

In fact I'd argue the opposite – that obnoxious articles like that aren't true fans anyway, just aggressive idiots looking for any excuse to kick off.

But, as I've said, it does seem that the trouble at the match itself was started by the Russians.

By the way, I'm playing the Cure's wonderful album Disintegration as I type. A bit earlier I was listening to a greatest hits collection by Fleetwood Mac (Stevie Nicks era in this case, but I also love the earlier stuff with blues maestro Peter Green).

This outstanding band had two distinctive phases. Both were exceptional and they're among my top 10 groups of all time – a very difficult achievement indeed as there have been so many brilliant outfits in rock history.

June 14 – Six England fans have been jailed after taking part in violent clashes at Euro 2016 in Marseilles at the weekend.

But French authorities admitted that an organised gang of about 150 Russian hooligans had escaped arrest after instigating the trouble.

England captain Wayne Rooney and manager Roy Hodgson have both appealed for supporters to enjoy themselves but not get involved in any fighting that could mean the team being sent home, robbing the country of the chance for glory after the players had worked so hard to reach the tournament finals.

There are grave fears that Russian and English fans finding themselves in the same areas of France will continue fighting, leading to both national teams being expelled.

On the field, an unfortunate own goal meant the Republic of Ireland ended up with a 1-1 draw in their first group game against Sweden after scoring first.

Reigning champions Spain beat the Czech Republic 1-0 and Italy notched up a 2-0 triumph over Belgium. England's next match is a crunch tie against Wales in two days' time.

In a mellow mood so I've slapped on a Bread CD. That sounds good, doesn't it? Crumbs!

June 15 – Musician Henry McCulloch, one time lead guitarist with Paul McCartney's Wings, has died aged 72. Apparently he never fully recovered from a heart attack four years ago.

Born in Portstewart, Northern Ireland, he appeared with Joe Cocker's Grease Band at Woodstock Festival and also played with Spooky Tooth, Marianne Faithfull and Donovan and toured with Jimi Hendrix and Pink Floyd.

But it is for his work with Wings that he will best be remembered. He played on their classic James Bond theme song Live and Let Die and was the man responsible for that brilliant guitar solo on the single My Love – often touted as one of the finest in rock history.

Continuing the mellow vibe, I've been playing the Carpenters.

In the footie, lowly Iceland, tournament minnows from the smallest country in the finals, pulled off a remarkable achievement yesterday by drawing 1-1 with the mighty Portugal, a highly-rated team featuring Cristiano Ronaldo, one of the world's best players.

Meanwhile, Russia has been told it will be thrown out of the competition if there's a repeat of the violence displayed by its (apparent) fans so far. The players are due to face Slovakia later today (Wednesday) in Lille – temporary home of English and

Welsh supporters in advance of that crucial match in nearby Lens tomorrow.

June 16 – Host nation France beat Albania 2-1 yesterday to secure their place in the last 16 and the knockout phase of the Euros.

In England's group, Slovakia beat Russia 2-1 to make it really interesting as England and Wales prepare for their game this afternoon.

Paul McCartney is 74 on Saturday, two days' time. I watched a You Tube documentary yesterday elaborating on the old claim that the real Paul actually died in a car crash in the 1960s and was replaced by a lookalike.

The hour and a half film was packed with what the makers alleged were clear indicators to this fact. Album cover artwork and Beatle song lyrics were among the cited pointers – especially when tracks were played backwards.

I consider this a conspiracy theory too far, even for me. I watched the movie feeling it would be absorbing, hilarious and highly entertaining. I wasn't let down. But it did make me think.

And the thought I had was, once again, the realization that we all have our blind spots and stubborn streaks when someone threatens our sacred cows, in my case the good old Beatles.

This is precisely why I understand others' resistance to some of my apparently weird, wild and wacky declarations. But we all have our opinions and beliefs you know.

June 17 – The nation is in shock after the murder of a female Labour MP yesterday.

Jo Cox, aged 41, was shot three times and stabbed in an attack just before 1pm in Birstall village, part of her Batley and Spen constituency, Yorkshire.

She was pronounced dead about an hour later, leaving her husband Brendan and two young children aged three and five.

A 52-year old local man has been arrested.

Jo Cox had only been an MP for 13 months. She was known as a passionate advocate of charity and justice working tirelessly for her constituents, who praised her as a woman of the people, not motivated by money or the selfish quest for power.

Brendan Cox is quoted as saying his wife would have wanted people to unite to fight against the hatred that killed her.

The motive for her murder is still a mystery but her alleged assailant is said to have shouted "Britain First" as he launched himself at her. Mrs Cox was promoting a vote to remain in the EU at next week's crucial referendum.

Campaigning on both sides of the debate has been suspended as a mark of respect amid fears her death will damage the "leave" group's chances of success.

Jo Cox appears to have been the right kind of MP – a decent and dedicated backbencher who saw herself in Parliament to represent the people, not feather her own nest.

I have no doubt there are many other MPs on all sides who are just as honest and honourable. In fact, many seem to start out that way but the ones that rise through the ranks to the top end up being greedy, self-serving, corrupt, ruthless, controlling, deceptive and cruel.

It's as if they become – dare I say it? – possessed. Physically or figuratively? Hmm.

In the football, England came from behind to beat Wales 2-1 and go top of the group with four points.

Gareth Bale drew first blood for Wales just before the break but Jamie Vardy equalized in the second half and substitute Daniel Sturridge scored the winner deep intro stoppage time.

I watched the match at the Bell with Penny and Nicola Williams, Laura and Mark and loads of mates – and it was great. The atmosphere was electric.

Later in the day, Northern Ireland notched up an impressive win over Ukraine to keep their hopes of making it to the knockout stage alive.

Been listening to some more melodic, mellow music – Al Stewart, Chris de Burgh, Cat Stevens and Crowded House.

June 18 – Happy birthday Sir Paul McCartney, 74 today. It's also the anniversary of my dear Mum's passing. Joy and sadness – the polar opposites of human existence, all wrapped up in one day.

Campaigning has resumed in the big EU debate. How bloody insensitive can you get? – The suspension of hostilities in respect of poor Jo Cox didn't last very long, did it? Disgraceful!

Thomas Mair, 52, of Birstall, Yorkshire, has appeared in court charged with Mrs Cox's murder.

In the Euro 2016 competition, reigning champions Spain are through to the last 16 and so are four times World Cup holders Italy, who have won the European trophy once, in 1968.

So that's hosts France, Spain and Italy all guaranteed to be in the knockout stage while there's still everything to play for in Group B, featuring England and Wales, and Group C, containing Germany and Northern Ireland.

The Republic of Ireland play Belgium in Group E later today with high hopes of also making it through to the next phase of the competition.

There are six groups, A to F, each with four teams making 24 in all. So therefore 16 will be going through to the knockout rounds while eight return home within the next week.

But the tournament was once again marred by trouble as hooligans claiming to be football fans started fighting and threw flares on to the pitch during Croatia's 2-2 draw with the Czech Republic, causing the match to be stopped for several minutes.

June 19 – It's Father's Day and Phil put a nice comment on Facebook for me, bless him. Emily joined in, calling me "Daddy Number Two", which was really cool.

For my own part, I put a photo of my Dad and Mum on Facebook with a little tribute to both of them. I've also lit a candle. I still miss them both terribly, even after all these years. It's a strange old weekend really.

As usual, I went to Sam and Carl's on Friday and stayed in last night, when BBC Four television broadcast the final of its UK Best Part Time Band competition, featuring the last six survivors out of the 1,200 groups starting out in the first round.

One of the outfits making it to the grand final was Bournemouth reggae band Dubheart, which I've seen a couple of times and love. I was chuffed to bits for these excellent musicians and their fans and I'm playing their superb album Mental Slavery as I type.

Speaking of reggae bands, I've secured tickets to see UB40 at Boscombe's O2 Academy in October and the Wailers – yes, THE Wailers – there in November.

Okay fair enough the only member of Bob Marley's original band is bass player Aston Barrett, but blimey! – This guy played alongside the legend himself, and there's no way Barrett would enlist second-rate musicians if he's safeguarding the Wailers' iconic name.

My very good buddy Jem saw Barrett's current version of the Wailers last year at the same venue and says they were brilliant. So I'm looking forward immensely to seeing them and UB40, who I saw at Poole three decades ago – one of the very best gigs I've ever been to.

I also have tickets for folk rock heroes the Levellers' gig at the local Academy in December.

That should be a blast, too.

June 19, 7pm – Just had a lovely Father's Day with the family. Phil and Emily brought Chloe and Harvey over to see me, armed with cards and home-made presents. They then took me out for a meal at the Commodore Hotel overlooking the sea at Southbourne.

After that, Phil drove us to their house in Ferndown to enjoy a couple of hours chilling with them, pet dogs Lola and Hamish and other resident animals watching a funny movie.

Em's parents Gail and Keith arrived, then Phil's mum Joe and her man Stuart – just as Phil and I were leaving so he could drop me back off home here. It was super seeing them all.

June 21 – It's the summer solstice and would have been Mum's birthday. I've lit a candle and put a brief tribute on Facebook.

Yesterday evening I went to the Bell to watch the England versus Slovakia game – a frustrating 0-0 draw but the one point gained means we go through second in our group to Wales, who beat Russia 3-0.

Our next match is next Monday evening and we wait with bated breath to see who our opponents will be – Hungary or Portugal, Iceland or Austria, who all play tomorrow.

This morning I went to Southbourne shops and while there I saw Bell landlord Mark Evans, sat having a coffee outside Costas. I stopped to join him for a cappuccino and a chat. Nice!

June 22 – Wishing a very happy birthday to my good buddy Steve Yarwood, 59 today. It should also have been Jo Cox's 42nd – a poignant thought as the arguments rage on in the last 24 hours before our crucial EU in/out referendum tomorrow.

Mrs Cox apparently wanted us to stay in and the man charged with killing her is said to have shouted "Britain First" as he attacked – the clear implication being that he desired a majority decision to leave and thought she was being a traitor to her country by advocating we remain.

Hmm. Is it just me who thinks this is more than a little suspect? – And all too convenient for some as it forces people to rethink their positions as they prepare to enter the polling booths?

As with the Orlando massacre, we need to ask the question – was the perpetrator a violent political extremist, insane psychopath or a brainwashed, mind-controlled patsy? Or even a ruthless undercover agent, possibly highly-paid, trying to stir up lethal bloodlust trouble?

Don't think that's possible? In that case I despair at your naivety and blind faith. It's a cruel and twisted world out there, especially where politics, religion or big business are involved.

Was Jo Cox – seemingly the right kind of MP, a thoroughly decent, diligent and caring woman with a big heart and kind disposition – a tragic victim of cold-hearted chicanery at its most evil, a nice person savagely sacrificed in a bitterly cynical attempt to sway the vote?

Of course there is another possible explanation – that she was simply very unlucky, not the intended target at all but in the wrong place at the wrong time as the armed man struck.

Who knows? As usual, the truth will remain shrouded in mystery and misinformation. But I do start to wonder when the alternative media says the guy reported to have overheard the gunman shout "Britain First" has since gone on record saying he heard nothing of the kind.

There's also a version where Mrs Cox intervened to try and calm a heated exchange between her attacker and another person. One thing's for sure – someone's lying and the whole sad and sorry story stinks to high heaven. We all feel for Jo's husband, children and community.

June 23 – Well referendum day has at last arrived. I've just been to the polling station at a local school to vote – and I put my cross, using my own pen, in the "out" box.

In the end, it was a very close call. I had deliberated for about a fortnight, unsure which way to go. When you stripped away the blatant lies and irresponsible scaremongering from both sides and considered the facts in a calm and balanced way, each made plausible, valid points.

The issue was nowhere near as clear cut as many tried to make out it was. It proved to be an extremely complex, multi-faceted matter and in the end posed a really tough choice.

Those who have read my books or heard me speak will know how much I despise the EU and the stifling power it has to incessantly over-ride our political, economic and legal systems.

I've detested the constant meddling of unelected bureaucrats in our country's affairs and the way they've dictated the high numbers of immigrants – or migrants – we've had to accept.

This is common sense, not racism. I hate the xenophobic, bigot mindset, seeing it as spiteful, divisive, hate-fuelled and ridiculous.

And I still think the relentless onslaught of the juggernaut super state is all part of an ongoing master plan to centralize power more and more in the hands of fewer and fewer people – an affront to the grass roots democracy I yearn for us to aspire to.

But I've long thought it's far too late to pull out now and we should have had this chance to vote two to three decades ago, before we became inextricably tangled up in the toxic EU spider's web. I fear to try and extricate ourselves now could seriously hit our economy.

So when Cameron announced in February that there would be a referendum, there was little doubt in my mind that I would reluctantly vote remain. Besides, that's Green Party policy and I'm a card carrying member who firmly backs its policies protecting people and the planet.

But as the big day approached I began to think that, as staying in was a done deal anyway regardless of the referendum's outcome, I might vote leave as my protest against the EU.

For weeks I wavered between the two options as both campaigns angered me by getting uglier, wilder, more deceitful and desperate as time started running out and rivals panicked.

I was especially appalled at the blatant scare tactics being used by both sides as facts and reasoned arguments were ousted by petty point-scoring and childish name-calling.

Then, with a week to go to polling day, Labour MP and remain advocate Jo Cox was killed and we saw the disgraceful and totally unconvincing attempt to portray her assailant as a right-wing racist nut, thereby discrediting the exit brigade.

For a few hours I actually considered voting remain, as a mark of respect for an MP truly worthy of the title and in an attempt to distance myself from hate-fuelled xenophobes.

Then I realized that's exactly what the manipulators were trying to achieve – a knee-jerk reaction from the public securing a victory for the pro-EU camp.

So in my case, the savagely cynical ploy very nearly succeeded but in the end, failed. It backfired big time by turning out to be the final deciding factor in swaying me to vote out.

After weeks of indecision and soul searching, I plumped for our leaving a power block I hate rather than stay in and try to transform it from the inside, as Greens across the continent want.

But I still maintain that, no matter what the referendum result is, we will be staying in – by hook or by crook. It's inevitable, and yet we're being presented with an illusion of choice.

Turning to football, the Euro 2016 group stage has finished with England, Wales, Northern Ireland and the Republic of Ireland all through to the last 16.

The Republic pulled off a sensational result by beating Italy 1-0 yesterday evening, a marvellous achievement that amounted to one of Irish football's best nights ever.

Wales and Northern Ireland play each other on Saturday (25th), the Republic face hosts France the following day and England line up against Iceland next Monday evening – all of them aiming to reach the quarter-finals.

I've been soaking up the sonic supremacy of some five-star classic rock albums on my stereo in the past few days – Abbey Road, Ziggy Stardust, Dark Side of the Moon, Goodbye Yellow Brick Road and the Doors' eponymous first album.

Dusting off Goodbye Yellow Brick Road again reminded me just how brilliant Elton John's great mate and main lyric writer Bernie Taupin actually is. In fact, he was one of my heroes and major inspirations when I decided to have a bash at it myself in the early 1970s.

Yeah, him, Bob Dylan, Chuck Berry, Buddy Holly, Paul Simon, David Gates (Bread), Peter Sinfield (King Crimson), Carole King, Pete Townsend, Ray Davies, David Bowie and the Beatle and Rolling Stone boys were the people who flicked my switch, song word wise.

Later they were joined by Joni Mitchell, Roger Waters (Pink Floyd), Kate Bush, Bob Marley, Lemmy and the Genesis, Black Sabbath and Led Zeppelin lads, Bruce Springsteen, Paul Weller, Joe Strummer and Elvis Costello and later still by Noel Gallagher and Eminem.

Like most lyricists, I admire and respect the literary genius of the all time great wordsmiths such as Dylan Thomas, Lewis Carroll, William Blake, Charles Dickens, Jane Austen, Mark Twain, Mary and Percy Shelley and William Shakespeare (or whoever it was who wrote the plays and poems attributed to him).

I just love the English language and the way people use it to paint vivid verbal pictures – especially when they're married to great music.

****

CHAPTER THREE

Uncharted Territory

June 24 – We're coming out of the EU! The results are in and the nation has decided, with 52 per cent voting leave and 48 per cent wanting to stay.

We're entering a new phase of uncertainty and change.

David Cameron, who spearheaded the campaign for us to remain in, stood outside 10 Downing Street this morning to announce to the world that he was stepping down, meaning the Conservative Party will have a new leader by the end of the year.

This is very good news for the nation. The not so good news is that his replacement as Tory top dog and Prime Minister might well be that embarrassingly eccentric oaf Boris Johnson.

The pound started to fall just before midnight as the first results came in, indicating that the exit brigade had done better than expected and the previous theory of a slim victory for the remain camp might be wrong.

This immediate impact on our currency suggested that the EU supporters were right in their prediction of an adverse effect on our economy if we voted out. But exit enthusiasts claim this was a temporary blip and the situation would soon stabilize itself.

Jubilant leave supporters are today celebrating the perceived return of power from Brussels to London, which they see as excellent news for UK autonomy, commercial freedom and border control.

But the remain ranks are downcast, making gloomy forecasts of monetary disaster and a significant loss of power, stature and security affecting all of us in very bad ways indeed.

It's a leap in the dark for sure and I am more than a bit apprehensive, even though in the end I voted out. The consequences could be beneficial or bring misery. I guess we must wait and see. But a huge plus is the halt of the oppressive EU super state juggernaut in its tracks.

We have just entered uncharted territory. Will there be another general election before long? How's our decision going to affect the pound, the economy, immigration control or the futures of our administrative and legal systems?

What effects will it have on jobs, housing, the health service, welfare benefits and the military? We just don't know. But then I'd argue the same would have applied if we'd chosen to stay in the EU.

Both options had their distinct advantages and disadvantages. It was a far more complex, multi-faceted issue than many tried to make out. A lot of people saw the referendum in terms of a single issue. It never was that simple.

Personally, I'm pleased that we've given both Whitehall and Brussels a clear indication that we deeply resent the control that's been exercised over all aspects of our lives by a remote, unelected, iron-fist regime wielding increasingly centralized power.

The future is unknown. But for the moment it feels so damned good that at last we're standing up for ourselves against the powerful elite running Europe and the rest of the world.

Economic concerns aside, there are of course two massive disadvantages of voting out. I've mentioned one of them already – Boris.

Imagine being associated with him. Worse still, imagine him running the country – ye gods!

The other, of course, is being on the same side as that other cringe worthy clown Nigel Farage, who has jointly spearheaded the exit campaign.

Nutty Nigel, leader of the allegedly racist and homophobic UK Independence Party, seems to be a modern-day Enoch Powell, blaming all our problems on immigrants – or migrants as they've been referred to all the time we've been in the EU.

Consequently, anyone who voices any concern at all over the unfettered influx of huge numbers of foreigners to our land is immediately branded a xenophobe as well.

I repeat, yet again, I share people's worry over this contentious issue but I ain't no frigging racist – quite the opposite. I despise racial, political, cultural and religious prejudice with a passion. And I detest the words of Farage and the hateful right-wing agenda he stands for.

June 24, just before midnight – I've had a good evening at Sam and Carl's with them, Rich Jeffery and Tina Mcauley. I grabbed a kebab and chips on the way home, ate them on arriving, went on Facebook then settled down for TV coverage of Glasto 2016, night one.

Headliners on the Pyramid Stage were the magnificent Muse. Now I'm watching the excellent dance/trance band Underworld, they of Born Slippy fame. Oh yes!

On my CD player this morning, I thoroughly enjoyed the albums Definitely Maybe by Oasis and Electric Warrior by T Rex. To once again pinch that line from rock star John Miles' classic song – "music was my first love and it will be my last." Amen to that, brother!

June 25, 6pm – Today is a very good day. Popped into the Bell earlier to attend its charity fun day in aid of animal charity the PDSA. A dog show, stalls and amusements were among the attractions and I saw an awful lot of lot of mates there.

Spent most of the session with Simon "Squeak" Turnbull and his lady Ruth Troke.

Just got home and had tea – vegetable soup, bread and Flora and wafer-thin ham slices – and now watching telly coverage of Wales against Northern Ireland at Euro 2016. Good game so far but no goals yet.

Earlier on, Poland beat Switzerland on penalties to secure their place in the quarter-finals.

Lunchtime, before the Bell visit, I watched ZZ Top's Glastonbury set on catch up TV. Later I'll be catching the live broadcast of bill-topper Adele's. This festival is literally, an A to Z of music. How damned cool is that?

July 26 – Adele was brilliant and Squeeze pleased. Other Glasto treats yesterday included Madness and the Last Shadow Puppets, featuring the Arctic Monkeys' Alex Turner.

Wales beat Northern Ireland 1-0 to reach the quarter-finals of Euro 2016. Portugal and Poland are also through and will play each other.

Heated arguments rage on as insults and recriminations intensify in the wake of the referendum result.

Cameron's impending departure has caused turmoil in the governing Tory party, now forced to find a new leader and Prime Minister amid loud cries from the public for another general election as soon as possible.

Poor Jeremy Corbyn, a Euro-sceptic put in an impossible position by being forced to take the party line – or at least that of leading Labour MPs – of remaining in, is being scapegoated in the most vicious and unfair way with demands he be replaced.

Social media has been disgracefully saturated with nasty and spiteful comments from both sides really laying into the opposing camp with a vitriol rarely seen even in that notoriously open freedom of expression medium.

Scottish National Party leader Nicola Sturgeon wants another independence referendum for her own country, where a large majority voted to stay in the EU, seeing it as better for them.

More people in Northern Ireland voted in than out but Wales had a majority calling for it to remain.

I say if the Scots want independence they can have it. The Northern Irish too, if they wish. Why not? It doesn't stop them being our very close neighbours, friends, allies and trading partners, does it? We're inextricably linked by blood and history and that won't change.

Of course, all this would have enormous ramifications for the United Kingdom, with England and Wales staying together and the others breaking away. Again, does this really matter if that's what the people in those places desire?

Personally, I'd welcome a reversal of the worrying trend to increasingly centralize power, ushering in a more grass-roots approach to democracy. As long as each nation – Wales and England included – retains a strong identity as a thriving sovereign state on the global stage.

As for the effects on the economy – jobs, prices and so on – I said ages ago that I feared exiting Europe could send it into a tailspin. I still do, but I'm hoping that if so, it's a short lived setback, things will soon stabilize and in the long run we'll all benefit and prosper.

There could be pain and misery in the interim, but we've already had that for years with Cameron and co – and he'd threatened more. I hope this is a fresh start and our beloved nations – all four of them – can finally regain their confidence and stride forward in the world.

I'm all for closer emotional and commercial ties with the Scots, Welsh and Irish, both North and South. Also France, Germany, Italy, Spain, China, Japan, Africa, Australia, the USA and the rest. But we don't need to give away all our political, financial, legal and military power.

Sure, some people voted out because they're racists. But these were in a minority and most of us have absolutely nothing against foreigners. We just wanted control of our country back.

And I would point out that, no matter what their leaders might claim, many people living in France, Germany and other European lands are just as nervous – hostile even – over the increased meddling of officious, overbearing unelected bureaucrats in their national affairs.

Especially when it comes to legal and administrative issues, political power, military matters and the migrant and refugee crises created by our leaders' callous and inept foreign policies.

A lot of them could now demand similar referendums. The EU could collapse. Good!

You don't have to be joined at the hip and tied to a treadmill to have unity of purpose – whether it's world peace, care of the planet or mutually beneficial trading agreements.

London Calling, that excellent album by the Clash, has been on the CD player as I write. Read into that what you will, but it was a choice I made because I hadn't heard it for a while, nothing at all to do with the events of the past few days.

And yes, I'm well aware that people in London, just like those in Scotland, Northern Ireland and Gibraltar, voted by a large majority to stay in the EU.

Having now come to the end of the Clash disc, maybe I should play some Proclaimers, Manic Street Preachers and Undertones to even it up? Nah – I fancy a bit of REM. The superb album Life's Rich Pageant in fact. And after that, the Hounds of Love by Kate Bush. Sweet!

June 27 – It's the anniversary of my dear Dad's passing today so I've lit a candle and mentioned him on Facebook.

I had a quiet night in yesterday watching the tail end of Glastonbury on the telly. Former Electric Light Orchestra front man Jeff Lynne filled the traditional Sunday tea time legends spot with aplomb, treating us to fine renditions of some of that band's most famous songs.

Then it was Ellie Goulding, Coldplay {with Barry Gibb) and Earth Wind and Fire. Splendid!

Other personal highlights of this year's festival included Adele, Disclosure, ZZ Top, Madness, New Order, Squeeze, Underworld, Jake Bugg, Muse and the Lumineers.

Coldplay front man Chris Martin drew an enormous cheer when he pleaded for peace and love in the wake of the tumultuous events and friction of the past few days. Spot on, Chris!

Labour and the Conservatives are both in meltdown with half the shadow cabinet quitting their posts and a new debate arising over who should be Tory leader and Prime Minister.

Former London Mayor Boris Johnson – an upper class twit if ever I saw one – seems to be the front runner. Good grief! I would have thought George Osborne would be a strong candidate seeing as Chancellors, traditionally PMs' right-hand men, often take on the mantle.

I hate the man's cruel, brutal stance but I wonder why he's been so quiet since Thursday, especially in light of the fact he's clearly an ambitious guy with his eye on the top job.

Maybe he's playing a crafty long game – letting Boris take the heat now and screw up so he can step in afterwards as the only credible alternative party leader and PM. He is shrewd.

Though not a big fan of Labour, I do feel that ditching Jeremy Corbyn would be a massive mistake. As I said at the time, I welcomed his accession as party leader because it meant at long ruddy last it had a man who could put up a credible alternative to brutal Tory policies.

In other words, a guy who didn't just look like a wannabe Conservative willing to sell out his soul and principles for a taste of power, like Blair and Brown had and Miliband could have.

But in the run up to the referendum, Euro-sceptic Corbyn had little choice but call for us to stay in because that's what most leading Labourites wanted. You know, the wannabe Tories.

Many of his grassroots party members actually wanted out of the EU, so Labour ended up as divided as the Conservatives on an issue that crossed party boundaries, over-ruling loyalties.

My own eventual decision to vote exit went against my Green Party's stance. It was far too important an issue to meekly follow the leader. It always was a matter of heeding your heart.

So it's a travesty that back-stabbing Labour MPs wanting us to stay in are now claiming Corbyn betrayed his party. His position was untenable. I have visions of snakes and rats.

On the Tory side, Osborne has this morning broken his silence – not to enter the leadership debate but to reassure us that in the short-term he will do his best to steady a rocking ship.

But he did warn that there might be pain as he tried to stabilize the economy, calm the markets and balance the books. Yeah, sure, I think we all know what that means – more of the austerity and cold-hearted control many exit voters resent. Like he needed an excuse!

Meanwhile, there have been more vicious and ugly statements on Facebook than I've seen over any subject – and it's got a lot worse since the vote results were announced. It's horrible.

I had hoped, rather naively, that once the referendum had taken place – no matter which way it went – we'd be able to put all the acrimony and bitterness of the recent past behind us and pull together to deal with the consequences, whatever they were.

The truth is they could have been dire, in different ways, whatever the people decided.

I'm both angered and saddened by the vitriol being spat out from both warring sides.

I'm with Chris Martin. Peace and love guys, unity of purpose. Let the spiteful politicians tear strips off each other. We're better than that. We share a great country – or rather, alliance of countries. Let's work side by side to heal the wounds and mend the splits. Please!

Otherwise, we're all bloody doomed. That's one thing we can be certain of.

June 27, 6pm – Been playing live albums by Muse and Coldplay today in the afterglow of Glastonbury – exceptional sounds! Also been watching M83, Wolf Alice, Tame Impala and Fatboy Slim's festival sets on catch up TV. Very good stuff!

June 28 – England are out of Euro 2016 – shockingly beaten 2-1 by Iceland yesterday after leading 1-0. Roy Hodgson has quit. It's a very sad, embarrassing day for English football.

I watched the match in the Bell with Penny and Nicola Williams, Mark Hemington, loads of other pub regulars and an old mate of mine called Pete Dowling. Great community spirit but a terrible result sparking anger and disbelief.

But, being English and displaying our optimistic bulldog spirit, we did launch into a drunken rendition of Monty Python's Always Look on the Bright Side of Life. It just had to be done.

So Iceland are in the quarter-finals, facing hosts France. Italy beat reigning champions Spain to line up a tasty tie with Germany. Wales are due to play Belgium. Come on you reds!

June 28, 6pm –Osborne is, predictably, inevitably and disgustingly, using the referendum result to threaten more austerity and public service cuts in a new Tory government.

Surely those elected to run our country – sorry, countries – have a duty of care to the people and a responsibility to put us first, shielding us from harmful exterior factors and influences?

It's far too easy and just plain lazy for our leaders to pass the buck and blame outsiders when attempting to justify their cruel and unfair policies that hit the most disadvantaged hardest.

Jeremy Corbyn is refusing to resign and says if there's to be a Labour leadership contest he will be in it. Good. I like him because he seems to be a decent bloke and a proper socialist setting out a real alternative to brutal Tory policies.

I also think that the Greens can work with him but never with hard line right wingers like Osborne. Corbyn echoes many principles we hold dear, Tories stand a million miles away.

And as a Green, I totally back his pleas for wounds to be healed; his continued zeal to fight against austerity and the strong desire he expressed to stay in the EU and try to transform it from the inside. That was very much my opinion until I very narrowly decided to vote leave.

June 29 – Turned on the TV news this morning to learn that a gun and bomb attack in Turkey yesterday had killed 36 people and injured more than 140.

Three attackers are said to have started shooting outside and inside the terminal at Ataturk International Airport, Istanbul, and then blown themselves up after police fired at them.

Prime Minister Binali Yildirim said early indications suggested that the so-called Islamic State terrorist group was behind the atrocity. As always, I keep an open mind. But it's awful.

Labour MPs have passed a vote of no confidence in Jeremy Corbyn, and candidates – including Boris – have been announced for the Conservative Party leadership contest.

Nasty insults and comments continue to be made in news broadcasts and on social media as the nation appears to tear itself apart amid warnings of catastrophe after the EU referendum.

Large foreign companies with sites in the UK are threatening to relocate abroad. Big business is panicking, it seems. But then, the tight control exercised by the EU, backed by a ruthless elite working through big business, was a major reason that some people voted out.

"It's Armageddon, we're all doomed. Now here's smiling Carol with the weather."

Pure instinct tells me that, at the end of the day, it's all going to turn out all right.

I don't wish to prolong the referendum debate. It's time to move on, deal with the situation we have and work together for the good of our country. But I will say one more thing.

It annoys me intensely that many are viciously turning on older people, claiming they all voted out knowing they're going to be okay, unlike the younger folk they've stitched up.

This is poisonous, divisive rubbish. My son and daughter-in-law, both 26, and most folk I know in their 20s, 30s and 40s decided out, whereas a lot of voters my age and older chose in.

And many of those now finding themselves in the verbal firing line actually fought a damned war to ensure that the youngsters now turning on them had the frigging vote in the first place!

****

CHAPTER FOUR

Healing The Wounds

June 30 – Happy birthday to my mate Tom Jones and Emily's mum Gail.

Well, it's a week on from you-know what. And what a week it's been! – Political parties in turmoil, a jittering pound, anger, recriminations, spiteful Facebook jibes, apparently racist attacks, physical assaults on exit voters and blanket coverage on the TV and in the papers.

Sickening violence, outrageous insults, graffiti and vandalism have been directed against Polish people and other ethnic minorities. It's abhorrent.

Hatred and intimidation have been aimed at MPs and citizens on both sides of the in-out divide. I wonder if it would have been this bad had the result gone the other way.

Somehow I doubt it, although the exit brigade would have had just as much cause for consternation as the remain side now seems to have.

I've got a horrible feeling that the physical violence and vitriol are each part of a sinister and cynical attempt to force an urgent national rethink, ensuring we stay in the EU after all – as planned. I did warn of this in my entry of June 9, two weeks before the r-r-no I won't say it.

While attempting to move on, I'm finding it so very difficult. Note to self – must try harder.

June 30, two hours later – Oh flippin' 'eck! Once again I feel compelled to comment on the fallout from last Thursday's significant event.

Exit advocate Michael Gove, one of those vying for Cameron's job, has really knifed Boris in the back by declaring that he "cannot provide the leadership or build the team for the task ahead." Nice bloke!

Gove was expected to back Johnson for party leader and Prime Minister after they fought side by side in the leave campaign.

His apparent betrayal means that current Home Secretary Theresa May is now the firm favourite – especially after Boris's subsequent decision not to stand and her own quite brilliant speech that's just been broadcast on the TV news.

I must confess I was both surprised and impressed. She'd campaigned on the remain side but said the people had spoken and she respected their decision. She stated firmly that there would be no second referendum under her leadership. Good.

She pledged to try and reunite the nation as a strong, confident presence in the world and a place to be traded with and invested in.

Exit from the EU would be slow but steady and a special department would be set up to handle this process.

She would include MPs from both sides of the EU debate in her cabinet in a bid to heal the party's own wounds.

May also ruled out a general election before 2020 in her bid to present herself as a calm, measured and reasoned leader intent on guiding our country into a peaceful and prosperous future. And she wanted that country to show itself to be both inclusive and tolerant.

Apart from the election bit, this was music to my ears. But then, even Cameron had rare moments when he made the right noises – only to show his true colours with his actions.

And I did notice she said nothing about her stance on the further austerity measures and public service cuts threatened by Dodgy Dave and Osborne. That's interesting in itself.

On the red side of things, Labour leader Jeremy Corbyn stands firm despite the no confidence vote and a challenge to his leadership from former shadow business secretary Angela Eagle.

I'm respecting Corbyn more and more as he carries on deflecting vicious verbal missiles with humour and grace. This man has principles and integrity – unlike many of his slimy and devious, self-serving colleagues.

And let's not forget that the no-confidence vote came from fickle, traitorous Labour MPs – champagne socialists, wannabe Tories – and he continues to have massive support from the party rank and file and trade unions. You know, the grass roots people, the oppressed ones.

July 1 – It's a Friday and another new month begins. It's also the 100th anniversary of the start of the Battle of the Somme.

More than a million combatants were killed or wounded during this massive five-month First World War clash, one of the bloodiest confrontations in all human history.

Remembrance services are being held at the French battlefield site and elsewhere. Quite right, too. Lest we forget folks, lest we forget.

Portugal beat Poland on penalties last night to reach the semi-finals of Euro 2016. Wales play Belgium today with the same aim – the biggest game in Welsh football since 1958.

Germany play Italy tomorrow and England's nemesis team Iceland line up against host nation France on Sunday.

I've been revisiting some more classic rock albums, courtesy of my CD player and stereo system – Aqualung, Broken English, The Queen in Dead, the Joshua Tree and Pilgrimage.

July 1, 11pm – It's actually my mate Carl Young's birthday next Tuesday, July 5th, but unfortunately he's working then so we had a party for him tonight, attended by me, Sam, Rudy, Bailey, Bec, Cameron, Tina Mcauley, Diane, Jem, Rich, Sonia, Steve, Ziggy, Albert and Bramble. Cool!

Wales have done it! – reached the semi-finals of Euro 2016 with a 3-1 victory over Belgium.

They now play Portugal on Wednesday evening, just one match away from the final.

Many congratulations manager Chris Coleman, Gareth Bale and the boys, you've taken your nation to its all-time high in the football world – and shown England how it's done in the process. All power to the mighty reds – Let's hope they go all the way and win the trophy!

July 3 – Happy 65th birthday to my "adopted sister" Suzette.

Comedy writer and actress Caroline Aherne has passed away aged just 52 after a battle with cancer. She was best known as her characters Mrs Merton, the irritating and nosy chat show host, and Denise in the Royle Family, which she wrote with Craig Cash who played Denise's husband Dave in that classic groundbreaking sitcom.

At least 75 people have been killed and about 100 injured in two bomb attacks in Baghdad, Iraq. Islamic State is reported to have said it was responsible.

A suicide car bomb exploded near a restaurant and shopping area in the central district of Karrada. Then a second bomb went off in the largely Shia area in the city's northern sector.

Shia and Sunni are two rival factions of Islam that have been locked in bitter, sometimes bloody conflict for centuries – a bit like Catholics and Protestants in Christianity.

This ongoing battle of ideas is the root cause of a lot of the violence and killing in the Middle East and elsewhere. The West's meddling, based on imperialism and a brutal, warped version of Christianity, has just further inflamed this dreadful and tragic situation.

Switching to a happier groove, Germany are in the semi-finals of Euro 2016 after beating Italy on penalties last night.

July 3, 4pm – And in an even happier frame of mind, I can report on a mighty fine few hours in the company of my son Phil and grandchildren Chloe and Harvey.

Daughter-in-law Emily had gone off to the tattooist with her brother Simon, so, at a loose end, Phil decided to pay his dear old dad a visit and bring along the grandkids. Sweet!

We had a coffee at mine as the children watched TV and re-arranged my flat. Then it was a stroll through Fisherman's Walk, where there was a mini-festival on with music, fancy dress, old cars and motorbikes and stalls.

Sunday lunch at the Commodore was followed by a saunter back through Fisherman's Walk, where I bought another hat and we saw my cousin Sandra and her long-time male companion Alan. Poor Sandy's not well at all – the big C – but she seemed in good spirits and revealed that they'd recently got married on the quiet. About time too, I joked.

Then it was back to mine for another coffee and chat. The family have just left.

Returning to the grim stuff, Bangladeshi Prime Minister Shiekh Hasina has announced two days of national mourning after an attack on a cafe in Dhaka left 28 people dead, including 20 hostages.

Most were killed with sharp weapons. Islamic State is said to have claimed responsibility.

July 4 – It's Monday, the start of another week and my parents' wedding anniversary. Bet they're still walking hand in hand in the afterlife.

France beat Iceland 5-2 to go through to the semi-finals of Euro 2016. They play Germany on Thursday, the day after Wales face Portugal. The final's next Sunday, July 10.

The match was on the telly at the Bell last night, where I saw Nicola and Penny Williams, Mark Chastney, John Gaynor, Matt

Brant, Louise Delahaye, Alex King, Demi Pitkin, Simon "Squeak" Turnbull, Ruth Troke, DJ Ross Maslin, bar staff Lottie Wragg and Dave Froud, Brian, Darren and of course guv'nors Laura Williams and Mark Evans.

It was yet another good evening in my local.

July 5 – Happy 52nd birthday to my mate Carl Young, as in Sam and Carl.

In the news, Nutty Nigel has bizarrely resigned as leader of the United Kingdom Independence Party. This seems to make no sense at all.

But let's not forget he stood down once before, after the 2015 general election, only to change his mind and carry on. That's how trustworthy the man is!

Farage is continuing as a member of the European Parliament he paradoxically fought to see the end of – another weird contradiction in this erratic and irritating buffoon's odd behaviour.

It's all very strange indeed and makes me wonder what on Earth is going on. I suspect smoke and mirrors yet again in this twisted Alice in Wonderland fake reality of ours.

After all, he and Boris jointly spearheaded the EU exit campaign which pulled off a sensational victory in the referendum. Both were in positions of great power and influence.

But both have now inconceivably decided to walk away – Farage from leadership of UKIP and Johnson from the Tory top dog contest he was odds on to win.

Don't get me wrong – I'm delighted to see the back of both these decidedly daft and potentially dangerous characters. I just find it all puzzling in the extreme, unbelievable and ultimately unsettling.

Seismic shifts are shaking our political landscape in the most radical way. Watch this space!

And speaking of the political landscape, the rise of internet communication had added a whole new dimension to the debates and dirty tricks that comprise a lot of it.

I've lately been watching You Tube documentaries mentioning Anonymous, a relatively new concept in agitation and protest.

Basically, it's a loose global network of activists – or rather hacktivists – using the internet, including social media sites, to promote freedom of speech and expression, ease of access to vital information and transparency in government, politics and big business.

The collective's slogan "We are Legion" refers to both the group's numbers and the chosen anonymity of its members. Although known initially for disruptive online pranks, it's become more serious in recent years.

One of the most recognizable features of Anonymous is the distinctive mask worn by supporters at protest marches and rallies. It's based on the face of Guy Fawkes, the feller known all over the world for his involvement in the 1605 attempt to blow up Parliament.

Fawkes is widely – but apparently wrongly – said to have been the leader of the gang involved in the Gunpowder Plot to establish a Roman Catholic monarchy.

The anniversary of this failed terrorist act is marked on November 5 with fireworks and the burning of a straw or cloth "guy" dressed in old unwanted clothes.

Some scholars now maintain that Fawkes was actually just a member of the gang, not the mainstay at all, but, just like Ronnie Biggs and the 1963 Great Train Robbery, he's subsequently become the most well-known participant and something of a folk hero.

People hiding behind the Fawkes mask have been seen at protest gatherings in London, Paris and all over, including the 2011

Occupy Wall Street demonstration in New York opposing greed, corruption and social and financial equality.

Anonymous has also hacked and disrupted internet outlets of Islamic State in response to murderous acts of terrorism.

Ironically, many well-known people have publicly backed the aims and campaigns of a network that relies on non-identification of individuals for its effectiveness in fierce and sometimes unlawful bids to fight for us, the people, against the ruling elite's callous control.

I myself am quite happy to go on record saying I much admire the protesters' ideals and intentions, but I draw the line at their more aggressive activities, especially the law breaking.

Keep it peaceful, disrupt by all means but don't endanger anyone. Only hit the power and pockets of those that deserve it, and stay on the right side of the law. That's my advice.

If you can do all these things, crack on!

July 6 – Yesterday being Carl's birthday, Sam and he decided to have a party, seeing as he'd managed to wangle the day off work after all. So I guess it was Carl's birthday bash part two.

Tina, Jem and Rich were there again, plus my good mate Darren Williams, who's also a long-time pal of Sam's.

I've referred to Darren in previous books, notably his having had a heart attack even though only in his forties. It was great to see him again and he gave me a big hug, which was nice.

It's funny – most times I see him these days he asks me if I remember a certain birthday of mine a few years ago now that involved alcoholic beverages at the Bell (where else?).

In truth I can't remember much about it at all because he and his mate Taz got me drunk on lager and a potent drink called Aftershock. He recalls it a lot more clearly.

Darren has read my books and always been very nice about them, so I make sure he gets a complimentary signed copy of each one as it comes out.

When he mentions Taz and that birthday, he queries why I haven't alluded to it in any volume of *Sunshine and Ice*. It's precisely because I can't remember that much about it.

But I decided to remedy the omission anyway – happy now Darren?

This morning's TV news told us that disabled South African athlete Oscar Pistorius has now been sentenced to six years in jail, not five, for killing his girlfriend Reeva Steenkamp.

An original conviction for manslaughter, for which he'd been sent to prison for five years, was overruled at an appeal hearing last December as the charge was altered to murder.

Pistorius, 29, was said to have shot Reeva four times through a locked toilet door at their home in Pretoria in 2013. He claimed he mistook her for an intruder and fired out of fright.

The six-time Paralympics gold medallist became a global track star by running on distinctive prosthetic "blades". His own legs were amputated below the knee when he was a baby.

His revised sentence could be changed again if either prosecution or defence take up the option of a further appeal.

July 7 – Happy birthday Ringo Starr, 76 today. Peace and love. I've put a photo of him on Facebook with a brief mention.

It's also, of course, the sad anniversary of the London Bombs in 2005. I put a little tribute to the victims on Facebook and will light a candle for them when I get home from the shops.

Wales lost to Portugal but can still return home with heads held high to a heroes' welcome after a magnificent run in the Euro 2016 in which they succeeded where England failed.

Classic albums reverberating through my flat in recent days have included Appetite for Destruction, Tubular Bells, Velvet Underground and Nico, Delirium, Back in Black, Leftism, Night Moves and 25 Years On.

July 8 – Lethal violence, thought to be racially charged, has once again rocked America.

Much of downtown Dallas, Texas, was in lockdown early today after snipers shot 11 police officers, five fatally, during a protest over deadly police shootings of black men elsewhere in the USA.

Three people were held in custody while a fourth suspect exchanged gunfire with authorities in a parking garage.

President Barak Obama, in Poland for a NATO meeting, condemned what he called a "vicious, callous and despicable attack."

July 9 – Had another booze and fun session round Sam and Carl's yesterday, with them, their boys, Becca, Cameron, Tina, Rich and Russell, who's our mate and Bec and Alex's dad.

July 10 – It's six years ago today that Mike Hannen, my buddy Jem's dad, shuffled off this mortal coil. Mike was a good bloke, amiable, funny and well-respected. Our thoughts are with Jem, his mum Bridget and their lovely family. I've lit a candle.

An update on the South Yorkshire Police scandal – Sir Cliff Richard is now suing the force and the BBC after they jointly orchestrated a televised raid on his Berkshire home in 2014 following child abuse allegations we later heard had proven to be unsubstantiated.

The 75-year-old pop star says his life was turned upside down. He's demanding, quite rightly, that people only be publicly named if and when criminal charges are brought.

There's a growing clamour for South Yorkshire Police to be disbanded. Long before this incident, officers faced serious allegations over their handling of the 1984 miners' strike and the

1989 Hillsborough disaster when 96 football fans died in a crush at an FA Cup tie.

Been playing the Beatles' brilliant White Album. Now listening to Motorhead's Orgasmatron. Nothing like your own personal rock fest on a Sunday morning!

July 11 – Yesterday was a sporty day. Portugal beat France 1-0 to lift the Euro 2016 trophy, Andy Murray clinched his second Wimbledon title and Lewis Hamilton won his fourth British Grand Prix.

Went to the pub last night where I saw Matt Brant, Jem Hannen, John Gaynor, Alex King, John Palmer, Dave Froud, Darren, Brian, deejay Ross Maslin, bar staff Demi and Emma and guv'nors Laura and Mark.

July 11, later – Theresa May looks like being our new Prime Minister after her last rival for the Conservative Party leadership, Andrea Leadsom, pulled out today, leaving the way clear for her to take the reins of party and country as preparations are made for us to exit the EU.

Born on October 1 1956 in Eastbourne, Sussex, May studied at Oxford before entering a financial services career including six years with the Bank of England.

She's been MP for Maidenhead since 1997 and served in various top shadow cabinet positions until being appointed Home Secretary in the coalition government in 2010 – a post she still holds.

On the other side of the Commons, Angela Eagle has indeed officially confirmed her bid to wrest Labour leadership from Jeremy Corbyn. She's his only rival so far.

July 12 – Happy birthday Lee Robertson, a drinking buddy of mine at the Bell.

David Cameron is to chair his last cabinet meeting as Prime Minister later today before meeting the Queen to tender his resignation tomorrow. So by the evening we will have a new PM –

our second female one in history. Maggie Thatcher, also a Tory, was the first of course.

May's appointment as Tory boss and our nation's leader has happened a lot faster than originally anticipated.

She's sounded refreshingly reasonable in speeches during the past couple of weeks. But on several previous occasions she's shown herself to be a typically brutal hard line right winger.

I guess we'll have to wait and see if she ushers in a new era of compassion, calm and common sense or turns out to be another cruel and callous Thatcher. I fear the worst.

Searching for truth is like peeling an onion. Just when you've stripped back one layer of perception, another appears and you feel compelled to keep on going.

The more we learn, the more we realize how far away we are from grasping the whole concept and seeing the entire picture.

Look at the aliens and UFOs issue. I was brought up to believe it was all fantasy, science fiction, too far-fetched to be true. Then I heard of the puzzling Roswell incident, Area 51 and Hanger 18, the odd inconsistencies and apparent cover-ups and I started to wonder.

Delving deeper took me into the decidedly weird world of seemingly outrageous conspiracy theory – David Icke territory. The whole ruthless reptile elite running the world thing.

Removing another layer, I learned that ancient religious texts and cave paintings from all over the globe told of humanity being seeded by visitors from the stars that bred with the resident homo erectus species and also artificially altered its DNA to form homo sapiens – us.

This was apparently done to quell a rebellion and make our millennia-old ancestors more docile and compliant – a slave race to do the donkey work as the reptilian aliens mined for gold to take back to their home planet, where it was badly needed for some reason.

Descendents of the alien/human hybrids that then became the world's rulers are still in charge to this day, while the rest us comprising the DNA-altered homo sapien slave race continue to be their viciously exploited subjects, it's claimed by some.

This does sound more than a tad unbelievable and the jury's still out on that particular aspect of the story as far as I'm concerned, but I am convinced that a rich and ruthless elite runs our world for its members' own benefit at our expense – whether or not they're reptilian aliens.

And let's face it; UFO simply stands for Unidentified Flying Object. Extraterrestrials don't necessarily come into it.

Strange airborne craft spotted acting erratically in our skies could simply be the visual evidence of top secret government experiments to master highly advanced technologies.

The 1947 crash in Roswell, New Mexico, could have been an accident involving one of these, veiled by various red herring theories including the allegation of aliens in a flying saucer.

Whether such futuristic technologies are extra-terrestrial in origin is a different debate. As always, I keep an open mind to all scenarios – even the apparently outlandish ones.

I'm playing the Beatles' A Hard Day's night album as I type. Seems appropriate, as it was released on 10 July 1964 (in this country that is – it came out on June 26 in the USA).

I've always loved it, from the first time I ever heard it all those years ago. It's in my top 10 all-time favourites list and is quite rightly recognized globally as the finest example of the beat music of that era, pop par excellence.

I still know all the words and every beat of those magnificent songs. This was early Beatles at their very best. A Hard Day's

Night was more a part of my education than most of the stuff I learned at school or church – fact!

Take a track like And I Love Her. There's nothing overtly clever, original or trailblazing about it. But its genius lies in its pure simplicity. Music teachers wanting to illustrate how to write the perfect pop song could easily use it in as an example.

The melody is beautiful; the lyrics are poetry at its most potent, direct and appealing and the musicianship outstanding in its stripped-back precision.

Like most Beatle songs, it's credited to Lennon/McCartney but we all know it's mainly Paul's. And yet the most outstanding and memorable feature is Harrison's guitar work.

Paul has used And I Love Her to illustrate how the group worked together to achieve the best results possible. "I didn't write that – George came up with it on the spot in the studio. But it became the song," said McCartney – or something like that.

July 12, 5pm – Just had a lovely afternoon in the Bell with Paula Carruthers, Nicola Williams, Mark Evans, Laura Williams, Alex King, Demi Pitkin, Dave Froud, pub puppy Flick and others. Cool as…

****

CHAPTER FIVE

Historic Changes

July 13, 6.30pm – I'm starting a new chapter, and so is the country. Cameron went to the Queen about an hour ago to tender his resignation as Prime Minister, followed by Theresa May, presenting herself to the sovereign as his replacement.

May then stood outside 10 Downing Street to assure us that she would represent us all, not just the rich and powerful. She would try and draw our divided nation back together again as a strong, positive presence in the world as we faced and tackled historic changes side by side.

The vicar's daughter, who attended a state grammar school before going to Oxford, was making a definitive effort to appeal to blue collar Tories in her bid to unite the people.

She made a point of saying she was leading the Conservative and Unionist Party and made it crystal clear she believed in that Union of England, Wales, Scotland and Northern Ireland.

Her first task is choosing her cabinet. Then she will spearhead withdrawal from the EU, plus of course the small matter of running the show in all other respects at the same time.

July 14 – Oh my stars! Very worrying news indeed – Boris Johnson is our new Foreign Secretary. Can you believe it?

One of the main reasons I was anxious when it looked like he was to become our new Prime Minister was the great fear he would spark an international incident.

For this clumsily-outspoken dolt is certainly no diplomat. He's come out with a string of ridiculous, embarrassing and insulting comments over the past few years.

He's been rude about both Europeans and Americans and once apparently likened current Presidential candidate Hillary Clinton to "a sadistic nurse in a mental hospital."

It will be interesting to see how he gets on with the White House and Continental leaders. Let's just hope and pray he doesn't cause a war!

The New York-born MP for Uxbridge and South Ruislip, a former Mayor of London, was, after all, one of the more irritating and offensive leaders of the "let's leave the EU" campaign.

So new PM Theresa May's appointment of him as Foreign Secretary seems bizarre to say the least. But the MP actually charged with handling our withdrawal is Secretary of State for Exiting the EU David Davis, heading a new department created especially for the major job.

Former Foreign Secretary Philip Hammond is the new Chancellor of the Exchequer in place of George Osborne, who's out of the loop completely.

Amber Rudd takes over May's old post as Home Secretary while Michael Fallon keeps his job as Defence Secretary. Liam Fox is International Trade Secretary, in charge of negotiating new deals in light of our EU exit.

Fox and Davis both advocated leaving the EU in the run up to the big referendum. So May, a remain campaigner, has kept her word in appointing ministers from both sides of the debate.

I'm listening to an album of Doors' songs, recorded in concert, as I write. Very good it is too.

This superb group is often cited by those claiming there's a demonic impulse behind rock music that will lead its fans into the arms of Satan and the fires of Hell.

Indeed, it's often been said that Doors' shows resembled perverted religious ceremonies with their charismatic front man, singer Jim

Morrison, leading the mesmerized masses like a possessed shaman. He even danced like one.

Morrison himself said he believed the souls of Native American Indians entered his body and took control when he was on stage.

And many of his song words resounded with aspects of black magic and blasphemy. He was a brilliant poet as well as a spellbinding master showman – the complete package.

Morrison and the Doors were mentioned in a documentary I watched on You Tube last night, made by a Bible-thumping Christian guy repeating the old allegation that rock music is a vehicle for Satan and an affront to God, who would send artists and fans alike to the fiery pit.

And the rest of the usual suspects were wheeled out to illustrate the point – the Beatles, the Rolling Stones, Black Sabbath, Led Zeppelin, Alice Cooper, AC/DC, Jimi Hendrix and so on.

I must agree that some of the lyrics are decidedly dodgy and the more outrageous and offensive antics repel me – especially those of people like Marilyn Manson, who seems to go out of his way to blaspheme and offend in the dubious guise of entertainment.

But Madonna, Eminem, Prince, Beyonce, Katy Perry and Adele have also been named as examples of those using phrases, actions, costumes and stage sets with diabolical themes.

I accept that many music stars – including John Lennon, Bob Dylan, Angus Young of AC/DC, Mick Jagger, Carlos Santana and Jimi Hendrix – have made similar comments to Morrison about become possessed and channelling otherworldly spirits or forces.

Does this make them demonic? Not necessarily. A lot of artists aim to entertain, excite, inspire and shock and none of it should be taken too seriously. I'd suggest that many provocative lyrics, statements, imagery and acts are employed with tongue firmly in cheek.

And the rebel in me loves this subversive impulse to shake things up a bit. In the end it's all relatively harmless – provided the fans don't respond in violent or destructive ways. You can't blame musicians for the activities of unhinged liabilities.

If it hadn't been songs and shows inspiring such loose cannons to top themselves or wreak havoc it would have been something else. Fact!

I watched the Christian feller's film with great interest and amusement but found some of his blinkered, rather conservative views unsettling – especially his clear dislike of gay people and anyone following an alternative spiritual path.

"But it's not me saying this, it's God, check the scriptures." Yeah right, the words of puzzled people trying to grasp and express deep divine wisdom, adding their own spin. So reliable!

A further thought also occurred to me – why do these smug, irritating, holier-than-thou bigots always seem to have annoying demeanours, dodgy haircuts and even dodgier moustaches?

I'll continue to check out all these weird and wacky You Tube presentations in my ongoing quest to gain wisdom and locate truth.

When it come to my own lyric writing, most of the time I'm well aware of what inspires me – a personal experience or one I've seen happen to a family member or friend, a news event, telly programme, movie, documentary, book or someone's song words, poetry or insights.

Occasionally I'm writing a verse or chorus and a line appears in my mind seemingly out of nothing and I wonder where on Earth it came from. I think of this as a thrilling form of magic, a spiritual force at work. But I've never felt I'm channelling anyone or anything else.

Maybe that only happens to the super-talented – the rare few special ones known for genius.

July 15 – Terrible news from France. A nutcase drove a truck into crowds watching Bastille Day fireworks in Nice yesterday, killing 84 and wounding scores of others.

The man at the wheel, said to be a terrorist, was shot dead after ploughing the vehicle through the festive crowd, sending hundreds fleeing in terror and leaving the area strewn with bodies, some of them children.

Authorities said they found guns and larger weapons in the truck, as well as identity papers belonging to a 31-year-old French-Tunisian citizen.

The country has been plunged into a fresh bout of trauma and mourning as the shockwaves have reverberated across the world. It's only eight months since the Paris attacks killed 130.

Once again it's being blamed on Islamic State and French president François Hollande has responded in defiant mood, saying the terrorists will never win and the country will strengthen its military role in Iraq and Syria in response.

Oh dear! – I've long argued that the aggressive foreign policies of Britain, America, France and other nations is probably a major reason for lethal Islamic radicalism in the first place.

I will never condone such murderous violence, which I despise with a passion, but it does seem to me that, rather than trying to find peaceful solutions, politicians appear to be Hell-bent on stoking the fires of division and bitter conflict.

And I'm convinced they're dancing to the twisted tune of the evil and ruthless elite running our world, our warped and bloodstained reality.

I stand firmly beside David Icke, Russell Brand, Anonymous and others in this.

Oh, and I find it very interesting indeed that this latest incident came just four days after the end of the Euro 2016 football tournament in France. Why not strike then, for maximum effect? It does make me wonder how much events are being orchestrated by sick minds.

A BBC correspondent, speaking on TV as I type, has just said that Muslims may well have been in that decimated crowd at Nice. Very good point! – Just goes to show that the brutal crazies responsible don't really give a toss about religion as they kill, maim and traumatize.

July 15, a bit later – Yeah, the sick-minded cash-obsessed, power-mad elite are the skilled specialists in getting us to suspect, hate and fight each other while they stay firmly in control.

They start and fund both sides of wars, create economic crises at will and exploit and manipulate us all, including our apparent leaders of every description, IS warriors and other violent extremists of all shades and colours.

Anyone believing passionately in any religious, political, ideological or cultural constructs is putty in the hands of these ruthlessly calculating lunatics whose savagely clinical cold-bloodedness is reptilian in nature, if not in fact. Some say it's both.

It's often asserted that all the power and money in the world is owned and controlled by the one per cent who relentlessly use and abuse the rest of us for their own selfish benefit. Well, the dark elite are apparently the one per cent of that one per cent.

Only they know all the details of the real game plan. Everyone else is fed various cover versions of the truth, the accuracy of which depends on how high up the pyramid they sit.

Most members of the secret societies these evil fruit loops work through have no idea what's being decided at the top. The onion analogy of layers of perception is so very apt here.

Some major politicians claim to be Christians, but their policies prove otherwise. Are they, in fact, Satanists, using a perverted, twisted style of Christianity as a smokescreen? Hmm.

Those last seven paragraphs sum up the firm convictions of a growing army of sceptics. And I must say that, as each day passes and more horrendous and baffling events unfold, it's increasingly becoming the only scenario that makes any kind of sense.

I've been playing the absolutely magnificent albums Rubber Soul and Abbey Road as I've been typing the last bit of this entry. Beatle reality trumps conventional reality every time!

July 16 – Wishing a very happy 40th birthday to my friend Kelly Millen, who's returned to Bournemouth from her new(ish) Yorkshire home for the occasion. Her son and daughter still live here plus many friends.

One of them is my very close pal Kerry Smith, 41 today. Happy birthday to you too, Kez!

At least 90 are dead and 1,500 soldiers have been arrested after a failed military coup in Turkey, a key Middle Eastern country at the world's ideological crossroads.

And it's now known that hundreds, not scores, of people were injured in the Nice lorry attack. Many are still in hospital as the nation starts three days of mourning. The guy at the wheel has been now been named – and described as a "weird loner". Yeah, another one!

A further case of mind control and brainwashing? Answers on a postcard please.

July 17 – It's Sunday morning and I've had another great weekend. Went to Sam and Carl's on Friday as usual for a bit of a session with them, Bec, Tina, Jem, Rich and Ryan Millen.

Last night I went to the Bell, where Kelly Millen – Ryan's mum – was celebrating her birthday. So was my friend Dawn Lewis, who's birthday is actually next Wednesday.

Dawn's best mate Penny was also there, plus Penny's daughter and Bell bar manager Nicola Williams, Nicola's feller Mark Chastney, Jem Hannen, Mark Hemington and John Gaynor.

Matt Brant, Alex King, Sarah and Darren Spence, Mark Evans, Laura Williams, Victoria Brown, Mark Thornton, Kelly Adams, Dave Froud, Krissie Benbow, Paul Clyde, Stu, Ian, Brian and Jim (don't know their surnames). Mates galore!

Today is my pal Jen Wheeler's birthday. Jen was given the nickname "Dottie" while working as a barmaid at the Bell a few years ago. It's stuck with people who know her from the pub at that time, and I wasn't alone in using it on a Facebook congrats message earlier.

Have a very happy birthday "Dottie!"

July 23 – Got back yesterday from a five-day break at a Weymouth caravan park with Sam, Carl, Rudy, Bailey, Bec, Alex, Russell, Cameron, Tina, Rich, Jem and four dogs – Blaze, Millie, Albert and Bramble. I thoroughly enjoyed it.

Meanwhile, in the outside world, bad stuff continues to happen. Nine people died, including the gunman responsible, after a shooting incident at a shopping mall in Munich, Germany. The attacker is said to have been a young man with dual German and Iranian nationality.

And Paula's just told me that her friend and work colleague Liz Waldron – a lovely lady with a gentle sense of humour – lost her husband to the Grim Reaper earlier today, her birthday. This is terrible and tragic. I've lit a candle.

July 24 – Islamic State has apparently claimed responsibility for a bomb attack on a protest march in Afghanistan yesterday.

Eighty people were killed and 230 wounded as two fighters detonated explosive belts at the Shia gathering in Kabul.

Thousands had come together to oppose installation of a new power line close to their homes.

News broadcasts late yesterday also carried more details about the Munich shootings. The perpetrator has been named as Ali David

Sonboly, 18, a loner (yep, another one!) with far-right political views.

It's claimed he targeted youngsters of Turkish or Arabic origins after being bullied at school.

I have little doubt this feller was an isolated, confused and troubled misfit, just like all the other sole assassins in high-profile attacks. But I feel the emotive term "loner" is deliberately used in such cases to strongly indicate independence in aims and actions.

There's a distinct possibility – likelihood even – that such unstable guys are actually targeted by bloodlust politically-charged organisations that then use brainwashing and mind control to get them to do the dirty work, sometimes creating a distraction. Crazed loner – case closed!

Also yesterday, our local football heroes, AFC Bournemouth – the Cherries – beat Portsmouth 2-1 in a pre-season friendly at Fratton Park. Sweet!

July 25 – Three little words can mask a world of pain and torment, misery and sadness – and they are "yes, I'm fine."

The glorious sunny weather that blessed our week in Weymouth, giving me a healthy tan on my face and arms, has continued over the weekend to today (Monday). So a bit earlier I sauntered through Fisherman's Walk to sit on a cliff top bench and gaze out over the bay.

I thought I'd make the most of the tail-end of the bright sunshine before the temperature drops and it turns overcast and wet, as the forecasters say it's going to do later today.

Yesterday evening I went to the Bell. Apart from Laura and Mark, I saw DJ Ross, off duty barman Mikey Delahaye and his mum Lou, John Palmer, John Gaynor, "Squeak" Turnbull, Alex King, Ollie Okoye, Lee Robertson, Brian and the on-duty bar staff Lee and Emma.

In the news, a failed Syrian asylum seeker is said to have fatally blown himself up and injured 12 other people with a backpack bomb in Ansbach, Germany.

Officials say the 27-year-old man detonated the device after being refused entry to a music festival. About 2,500 people were evacuated from the venue after the explosion.

While typing this I'm listening to Iron Maiden's Book of Souls. It's yet another ambitious departure for them – this time a full-blown themed double album. And it's very good indeed.

I've always considered Maiden to be a cut above the average heavy metal band and this long player proves it. From day one they've always displayed refreshing levels of imagination in their song writing, setting intelligent lyrics to fine melodies and playing them with great skill.

And their live shows are outstanding. I've had the great pleasure of seeing them three times.

The first was at Bournemouth Winter Gardens on the Killers tour (with original singer Paul Di Anno), the second at Poole Arts Centre on the Number of the Beast tour (with Bruce Dickinson on vocals) and the third, same venue on the Powerslave tour (Bruce again).

In fact, Dickinson has been with them ever since, right up to the present day, as they've grown into a massive global success story with incredibly passionate fans all over the place, from Germany to Mexico, Japan to Brazil, Australia to Italy.

July 26 – Oh blimey! Yet another murderous and merciless slaughter of innocents, this time in Japan.

A 26-year-old man is in police custody after a frenzied knife attack on a care home near Tokyo earlier today that killed 19 residents and injured 26, most of them badly.

The man, who apparently handed himself in after the stabbings, is claimed to have worked there previously and to have said he hated disabled people, wanting them dead.

This is deeply shocking – a truly sickening sign of our increasingly violent times.

Meanwhile, in our own country, the huge American internet-based retail company Amazon has won government support for its plan to deliver goods using drones – unmanned aircraft.

Currently, millions of people all over the world order all manner of items online and have them brought to their doors by vans. Drone drop-offs are seen as the future.

The Civil Aviation Authority has granted Amazon special permission to test its aerial vehicles without several of the rules that normally restrict drone operations.

This is being presented as an exciting development, offering the chance to have goods in shoppers' hands within half an hour of ordering rather than the next day as at present.

But I'm sure I'm not the only one worrying that the relaxation of airspace rules to aid commercial companies could be used to increase unwanted intrusion into our private lives.

Especially when an Amazon spokesman was on the telly this morning assuring that the company was not interested in surveillance, only in enabling faster deliveries.

Why the Hell did he even feel the need to say that? He could have just emphasized the second part of his comment and not even mentioned the first. All he's done is increased suspicion!

Let's face it, we already have no idea of the levels of government-backed or private company spying we're being subjected to through various means including the skies and the internet.

George Orwell was spot on with his novel *1984* and its predictions about Big Brother watching our every move. Was he a visionary – or an insider? Makes you wonder, don't it?

Been playing Blockbusters, a Sweet compilation album, while writing this entry.

July 26, 4pm – Just had another super session at the Bell, with Laura, Mark, Nicola, Demi, Harry, pub puppy Flick and others. Very nice!

July 27 – An 84-year-old priest was killed and four people taken hostage as two armed men stormed a church in Rouen, France, yesterday.

It's claimed that the attackers, said to be from Islamic State, slit the clergyman's throat during morning mass.

Police surrounded the church and shot dead both men. One hostage is critically ill in hospital.

July 28 – Wishing a very happy birthday to my very good pal Sam Excell. Hope you have a good one girl, see you tomorrow to celebrate. Birthday wishes also go out to my mate Steve Elvidge – nutty Steve from that mad, legendary Devon holiday mentioned in Volume One.

Well, we've had a bit of rain but the weather's still generally very warm and sunny.

July 31 – It's Sunday and I've had a mighty fine weekend. Friday I went to Sam's for her belated birthday party – sweet! – And yesterday we had a family fun day at the Bell in aid of the Homes for Heroes charity for homeless ex-service personnel. It was simply super!

It was great to see my mates Tina and Jeff McNally again and there were so many other familiar faces there I won't attempt to list them through fear of leaving someone out. Suffice to say I had many people to chat to and have a laugh with. The live music was good too.

Yes, I'm having a ball at the moment but I do remain acutely aware that not everyone is lucky enough to be in the same boat. Sadness, pain and misery continue to inflict people all over the world, including some of my nearest and dearest. It's a tragic fact of life.

I've had my share in the past, and no doubt more will lie ahead. But for now, things are cool.

Oh Gawd! – There's been yet another shooting in America. A woman in her 30s is dead and three other people in hospital after the attack in Austin, Texas. So far details are sketchy.

Isn't it about time gun licensing laws over the pond were tightened? This is getting way out of hand!

Also in Texas, about 30 miles from Austin, a hot air balloon caught fire and crashed killing all 16 people on board in the worst such incident in US history. Bad news!

Better tidings are that Belfast's Carl Frampton, 29, is the new WBA world featherweight boxing champion after beating title holder Leo Santa Cruz on points in Brooklyn last night.

It's a bit of a golden era for UK pugilists – we currently have 12 world leaders, including Frampton, Tyson Fury (WBA heavyweight), Lee Selby (IBF featherweight) and Lee Haskins ((IBF bantamweight).

I don't really like boxing but it's nice to have so much success in any field of endeavour.

Also in the news, some American idiot chucked himself out of a plane without a parachute and plummeted 25,000 feet into a giant net.

Luke Aikins' massive daredevil leap got him into the record books as the first man to skydive that far minus a chute. Why? Beats me – because he's nuts? Brave but barmy I'd say.

The 42-year-old's spectacular stunt over the Californian desert was broadcast live on Fox TV.

July 31, several hours later – I've just seen a fascinating but outrageous You Tube presentation claiming the whole enterprise was a deadly serious and highly symbolic display of the tightening grip of Illuminati/Satanic power over our world. Really?

The documentary makers pointed to the fact that the guy's name Luke means bringer of light, same as Lucifer, and the plummet was even billed as Heaven Sent.

They also said that numerology – the importance of numbers – was written all over the big gesture. Aikins was a veteran of 18,000 jumps – six plus six plus six, the sign of the Beast.

The stunt took place on the 30th day of the seventh month – three and seven being sacred numbers.

I know, I know, it all sounds very tenuous and more than a little crazy. But then it's often said that members of the Illuminati, or whatever the dark cabal ruling our planet's called, are totally obsessed with numerology in orchestrating events across the globe.

Some claim that one of the most blatant examples of this was the London Bombs – on the seventh day of the seventh month in 2005 – two plus five equalling seven again. And 911 as well of course – 11 being another powerful number and nine being three times three.

The dates of many other terrorist attacks and similarly significant occurrences are quoted in this context. Fanciful notions? Mad conspiracy theories? Or pure coincidence? I wonder.

But I do firmly believe in the magical power of numbers, ratios and sacred geometry – as evidenced in the Giza Pyramids, ancient and modern architecture, widely in nature and even in the human body, including our DNA.

August 1 – I've been thinking about swimming lately. Not to take it up again myself, you understand, but remembering fond recollections of when I did.

It's probably because I know pals of mine have been taking to the water in recent times. My own swimming days are behind me – I never was comfortable about stripping off in front of others and I'm even less prone to now. Unless it's in an intimate situation with a lady, that is.

I'm chuffed to bits that I was the one who gave my son Phil his last bit of confidence and advice to help him master the activity.

It takes me back to when my own Dad did the same for me. The remarkable thing in his case was the fact that he did it from the sidelines, too self-conscious to shed his clothes due to a severe case of the skin condition psoriasis.

The massive irony was that when he was in hospital with cancer, the staff found him pills and potions to clear it up. So he died with near perfect skin after a lifetime of discomfort and embarrassment.

August 2 – It grieves me greatly that I've upset one of my closest, dearest, longest-standing friends. I handled a delicate situation badly, letting them down, and it seems it's too late now to make amends and repair the huge damage. Apologizing hasn't worked. It breaks my heart.

A manhunt is underway after the Austin shootings at the weekend. It's believed one guy went on the rampage in several incidents.

August 3 – Had another lovely afternoon in the Bell yesterday with my very good friend Paula Carruthers. It was our four-weekly drinks and catch-up session.

Laura was there with her puppy Flick plus bar manager Nicola, who wasn't well so went home after doing the staff rotas. Krissie Benbow, Ben Avill and "Squeak" Turnbull turned up a bit later but pub landlord Mark was away for the day.

August 4 – More violence, this time on home soil. A woman in her sixties was killed and five other people injured in a knife attack in Russell Square, London, last night (Wednesday).

Police fired a stun gun as they arrested a 19-year-old man at the scene. He was taken to hospital where he remains in custody. Mental health issues are cited as a significant factor but terrorism hasn't been ruled out.

A very dear friend has recently questioned my loyalty – and that hurts, a lot. I know I can be a crap mate on occasions and I wish I wasn't. But I guess it depends how you define loyalty.

To some, showing loyalty means you're constantly at their beck and call, always dancing to their tune and indulging them way beyond normal, acceptable limits.

To others, it represents eagerness – ferocity even – to get involved in their fights and side with them against someone you have no quarrel with.

Others still have unrealistically high expectations of their nearest and dearest when tragedy or disaster strikes. Thinking about it, I guess we all can. We need to cut each other more slack.

But I don't go along with any of these definitions. To me, loyalty is showing love and concern, letting your family and friends know you're always there to help pick up the pieces – albeit sometimes in a limited capacity and from a distance.

I've been playing the albums Love by the Cult, Jubilee by the Sex Pistols and Idol Songs by Billy Idol.

August 6 – The 2016 Olympic Games opened in Rio de Janeiro, Brazil, a few hours ago, which was the early hours of the morning here due to the time difference. Here's hoping our athletes excel themselves and do us proud!

I went to Sam's yesterday for our usual Friday booze and laughs session with her, Carl, Rudy, Bailey, Tina Mcauley, Rich Jeffery, Becca and the mad mutts Bramble and Albert.

At least 13 people died and another half dozen were injured in a blaze at a birthday party in a bar at Rouen, France, last night. Candles on a cake apparently set fire to the room.

Happy birthday big Sam – Kevin Sansom, an old Bell buddy who's moved away. Have a blinder mate!

August 7 – And happy birthday Tina Wilkins, another old Bell drinking pal who now lives elsewhere in the country.

Last night was excellent! I saw two other former Bell regulars, Paul Dangerfield and Sarah Garbutt (formerly Basham), back at their old local. They're holidaying in Dorset from Wexford, Ireland, their home for the past 12 years or so.

Sarah and Paul drew a large number of their old Bell and White Horse chums and it turned into a bit of a reunion party with Tina and Jeff McNally, John "Brun" Smith, Rod Marlow, Gary Preston, Mark "Tich" Hemington, Amy Wrixon and Sam and Dave Lowney.

Plus Jem Hannen, Matt Brant, John Palmer, Penny Williams, Dawn Lewis, John Gaynor, Billy Clarkson, Mark Thornton, Krissie Benbow, Paul Clyde, Jim, Brian, Aussie Stu, Sarah Spence and her hubby Darren, our UK karaoke champion rocking his local watering hole.

It was brilliant – but unfortunately tinged with profound sadness due to the breakup earlier in the day of a long-standing couple we all know and love. The lady was at the pub and in tears.

A world record but no medals – that's Team GB's story after day one of the Rio Olympics.

Derby lad Adam Peaty, 21, broke his own world record to set a brand new one with his lightning fast swim that won his heat and put him in the final of the 100 metres breast stroke.

We had a couple of close calls where our competitors very narrowly missed out on bronze medals. But that was it. Very early days though – and Peaty must be favourite for gold now.

It's often said that millions of people can't be wrong. Well, yes they can – of course they can, if they've been bombarded with lies, deluged with propaganda and spoon fed a false reality.

In this respect many so-called conspiracy theorists point to an organisation called the Tavistock Institute of Human Relations, seen as a key component of the sinister New World Order/Illuminati agenda.

Wikipedia tells us that this London-based initiative, set up in 1946, is a British not for profit body concerned with group behaviour.

But opponents such as claimed former MI6 intelligence officer Dr John Coleman, say the Institute has systematically brainwashed folk and manipulated British and American public opinion to back two engineered world wars and the Vietnam, Afghanistan and Iraq invasions.

There are even assertions that it created Beatle mania and the destabilising seismic shifts in paradigms and attitudes during the 1960s, referred to as the Aquarian Conspiracy. Really?

I say so-called conspiracy theorists because I'm growing to hate the term. It seems to have become a widely used alternative to words like nut job and fruit loop, a lazy way to ridicule or discredit anyone daring to question any aspect of the brutal game plan being forced on us.

As I've said before, I don't entertain all these seemingly outlandish notions but I feel there is validity in some of them. I keep my mind open – that way it's harder to influence and control.

If something sounds right and makes sense, I'll consider it as a possibility, likelihood even.

I suppose we can't really talk about brainwashing and mind control without mentioning Laurel Canyon, MK Ultra and Sandy Hook.

The leafy Hollywood suburb of Laurel Canyon was the epicentre of American hippie counter culture in the 1960s and early 1970s, launch pad of the Byrds, Frank Zappa, Buffalo Springfield, the Mamas and the Papas, Joni Mitchell, James Taylor, Jackson Browne, Linda Ronstadt and the Eagles. Jim Morrison, lead singer of the Doors, also lived there at one time.

Before that, it attracted big film stars including John Wayne, Marilyn Monroe and James Stewart. But it was also the backdrop for the shocking, blood-drenched Manson murders.

And there are allegations that the whole hippie scene was created by the CIA as a social experiment. It's certainly true that Morrison and several others had parents in the military.

Nothing sinister there, you might say, and in fact it could be reasonably argued that it was precisely because their backgrounds were so embedded in the conservative establishment that they rebelled against it so vehemently.

And the rock stars probably grew up together if their families moved in the same circles on military bases and suchlike. Again, nothing out of the ordinary there.

But closeness to the military might well have gone hand in hand with exposure to potential secret service and intelligence agency manipulation. It's not beyond the realms of possibility.

Laurel Canyon might even have been a project of the notorious MK Ultra mind control programme said to have experimented on human guinea pigs to test drugs (including the hallucinogen LSD) and procedures for use in interrogations and torture.

It was a CIA initiative and some claim it was used – and continues to be used – to brainwash and control the minds of so-called lone wolf assassins in high profile murder cases.

Which brings us to the massacre at Sandy Hook Elementary School, Connecticut, in December 2012. Adam Lanza, 20, was said to have shot himself dead after gunning down and killing 20 children and six staff members.

But inconsistencies in the official story have led some to believe Lanza was mind controlled and the whole thing was a secret services set-up to test public reactions to such a tragedy. It was an elaborate hoax and no-one died at all, they assert.

I'm in no position to boldly or arrogantly say if any of this is true, and I do accept that all three topics seem so far removed from normal reality to be positively beyond belief. But that reality is false. I'm just putting them out there and inviting readers to decide for themselves.

Today's news includes the shocking tidings that at least 52 people have died in a bomb blast at a hospital in Quetta, Pakistan. No-one has yet claimed responsibility.

At the Olympics, Adam Peaty did indeed win gold, once again breaking his own world record. Minutes later, fellow swimmer Jazz Carlin, 25, of Swindon clinched silver in the women's 400 metres freestyle – Team GB's first two medals in Rio.

August 9 – You've probably gathered that I've recently discovered the delights of You Tube through my telly.

This is not only great for catching loads of intriguing reality-challenging programmes you'd never see on mainstream TV, it's marvellous for accessing brilliant songs I don't have on any of my CDs.

Tracks like the kickass Prime Mover by Zodiac Mindwarp and Sister Seagull by Bebop Deluxe, and the beautiful Will You by Hazel O'Connor, Hairless Heart by Genesis, Sea of Joy by Blind Faith, Persephone by Wishbone Ash and The Recollection by Rick Wakeman.

Plus the magnificent Nantucket Sleigh Ride by Mountain.

I also have Shadow Play by Rory Gallagher, Badge by Cream and Medicine Jar by Wings on my You Tube history list, although I also have them on CD.

And I can play my TV through my stereo system to get a full and rich sound. Excellent!

****

CHAPTER SIX

Pyramids

August 10 – Had another nice afternoon in the Bell yesterday with Laura, Mark, Nicola, Alex King, Paul Clyde, a guy called Pete and new barman Tony Jeffery, my mate Rich's son.

It's very appropriate to be in the pub right now as Laura and Mark celebrate the two year anniversary of its relaunch as the Bell.

A new craze called Pokemon Go is sweeping the globe. It's a game that asks participants to find computerized virtual reality characters in real-life locations using their mobile phones.

All jolly good fun, you might think, but there are some who claim it's not the harmless pastime it's made out to be and is in fact worryingly sinister and potentially very dangerous.

Pokemon Go has become a smash-hit sensation since being launched in mid-July with millions of all ages worldwide getting zealously involved.

There have been stories of people walking into traffic and falling off buildings because they've become so deeply engrossed in the highly addictive game that's proven such a major distraction from the real world and all its problems. Some would say this is part of the point.

But they go further, highlighting the fact that in order to play you have to give the game's operators, a firm called Niantic, access to your phone-held facilities including its camera.

This means that at any time your exact location (even indoors), who you're with, what you're doing, highly personal pictures and videos, your e-mails, text messages and all phone-held information about you are available to the private company.

This could all be perfectly innocuous, but questions have been asked about how this data might be used – especially when Niantic's own terms and conditions state that it co-operates with governments, law-enforcement agencies and other private firms in sharing information.

In these days of Google Earth, Facebook and Twitter, this is seen as an alarming new level of surveillance and intrusion into people's privacy. Big Brother spies know more about you than many of your nearest and dearest, including some highly sensitive details, it's claimed.

Careful what information you release to the Internet, because we're all being constantly tracked – and more effectively than ever with Pokemon Go, warn the suspicious and anxious.

Blimey! I'm so glad I don't play such computer games! But I am on Facebook and Google Earth. Certainly makes you think, don't it? – Especially when some Facebook users have hilariously but quite cynically and ruthlessly taken the piss out of such legitimate concerns.

August 11 – Happy 23rd birthday to pub landlady Laura Williams. Have a great one girl – you deserve it for the terrific work you and Mark have done making the Bell a huge success.

Pyramids are so crucial to our civilisation, don't you think? They can be seen all over the world as potent religious symbols and representations of perfection and the golden ratio.

But they're also a crucial feature in the whole structure of our societies.

There are pyramids of power everywhere, with one big chief at the top and the various levels of the hierarchy spreading out and down to the numerous humble minions at the base.

Two of the most obvious examples of this are the military and big business. But it's true of government, the monarchy, education, organised religions, the media – in fact, everything.

And our world community itself is one huge pyramid. But who sits at the top of this mother of them all is open to speculation and debate – the tip is so high up, shrouded in mystery.

We have individuals, neighbourhoods, towns, cities, regions, countries and power blocks of countries such as the European Union, the North American Union (the USA, Mexico and Canada), the African Union and the Asian Union of China, Japan, Australia and others.

A growing army of folk are saying that the move to a one world government, army and religion – the New World Order – will involve the end of nations and the eventual merging of these massive power blocks into a single global super state, sooner rather than later.

The UK's recent shock referendum vote to leave the EU seems to have thrown a spanner in the works. But I still say it's only a temporary glitch.

Much as I hate the overbearing meddling and undemocratic centralization of control – I voted out, just – I'm sure that us being part of a Euro power block is inevitable, one way or another.

The pyramid structure prevalent throughout human society means that it is indeed possible for a tiny minority led by one person to rule over us all – possibly with an iron fist.

Few could argue with the logic of this, but supporters of the one world idea say it could stop wars and usher in a new golden age of co-operation and peace. It's a lovely idea and an ideal that the peace loving, optimistic hippy in me fully supports. But there are grave dangers.

And these arise from a deep anxiety over the nature and motives of those in charge of this potentially utopian society. It could so easily result in a nightmare global fascist state where democracy and human rights are demolished as billions of us become slaves to the few.

The one single army would be there to brutally enforce the laws passed by this tiny elite.

Many claim we would be totally controlled robots, constantly being led and tracked, scared stiff to step out of line for our own sakes and those of our loved ones. I fear they're right.

I'd say we're well on the way to that already. Disagree? – take another look around you!

Speaking of ideals brings me to environmental issues and my membership of the Green Party.

My decision to join was based as much on the organisation's stands on democracy, decency, honesty and looking after people as its obvious zeal to protect our planet and wildlife.

I fully support the party's compassionate anti-austerity agenda demanding social justice and fairness, putting human beings first alongside animals, plants and our nurturing Mother Earth.

We have recklessly plundered and destroyed Her resources for far too long. To continue to do so would rob ourselves of our own vital sustenance – suicide!

Some claim global warming, or climate change, is a myth – another bid by the unscrupulous bastards in charge to mess with our heads and manipulate us into supporting their own self-serving, sod the rest of us savage agendas.

I'm not sure one way or the other on this particular point, but no-one could justifiably or sanely argue against the devastation we've inflicted on our environment and wildlife.

And the severe damage we've done to our home planet we so heavily rely on for our very survival is often quoted as a good reason to halt population growth before it threatens us all.

Some horrible people have even gone on record saying that throughout human history major wars have served to keep populations down and now we need other ways of achieving this before it all spirals out of control with dire consequences for our species.

Enforced birth control, mass sterilisation and even killing off billions with man-made global epidemics have been suggested by evil whack jobs in positions of great power. Bloody Hell!

I can certainly see how people's justified concerns over the environment could be used to persuade them to back population control measures.

Social engineering in this form is called eugenics. Hitler's version of it was extreme ethnic cleansing resulting in mass murder in the Nazi death camps.

I also suspect there could be at least some truth in allegations that the discovery of life-saving drugs and procedures might have been suppressed – also in a bid to keep populations down.

This raises one obvious question – Has a cure for cancer actually been found? If so, that's as truly despicable and shocking as the claimed suppression of environment-friendly energy systems and sources by those with vested interests in lucrative but fast-dwindling fossil fuels.

That's both nuts and evil – holding back progress for your own selfish short-term gain, or in the case of eugenics, to serve a twisted and widely lethal agenda.

Gordon Bennett we've got heavy, haven't we? Or at least I have – you've just been reading my deranged prattle. Time to lighten up, methinks.

Kayaker Joe Clarke and diving duo Chris Mears and Jack Laugher won gold as our athletes doubled their medal tally to 12 within 24 hours on day five of the Rio Olympics yesterday.

So we now have four gold – and yesterday's bronze medals in cycling, shooting, judo and gymnastics also helped lift Team GB to ninth in the table, led by the USA, China and Japan.

Been playing CDs by Simple Minds, Mike Oldfield, Coldplay and the Happy Mondays.

August 12 – Four people have been killed and several injured in a series of bomb blasts across Thailand.

Four devices exploded in the town of Hua Hin within 24 hours and several more went off on the island of Phuket. No-one has yet come forward but separatist insurgents are suspected.

Resort areas seem to have been targeted and the timing is sensitive – today being a national holiday marking the Thai queen's birthday.

In Rio, Great Britain has risen to eighth in the table with 16 medals and more expected to come today. The United States leads the pack with 38, followed by China and Japan.

It's often said that the dark elite at the top of the global human pyramid, manipulating all sides in wars and crises for selfish ends while staying firmly in control, works largely through secret societies, using strong but clandestine connections to further its evil agenda.

Of course the largest and most famous secret society in the world is Freemasonry. Sure, most people have heard of it and know of its tight bonds of loyalty, odd handshakes and rituals.

TV dramas, films and novels have frequently told intriguing stories of corruption, deceit and shady practices being enacted under the cloak of confidentiality the organization so relies on.

Millions of recruits use it as a mutually beneficial brotherhood where members help each other succeed while raising shed loads of cash for charities. Great I say – if that's all it is.

But there's widespread evidence of the savage treatment of outsiders in order to benefit the members. The government, judiciary and police – all said to be full of Masons – are often accused of covering up their brothers' crimes, framing others and using them as scapegoats.

The vast majority of members occupy the bottom three levels of the Masonic pyramid. But it's said there are 30 other higher ranks and each step up reveals more of the society's inner workings and real purpose. And that's said to be very dark and twisted indeed.

Me? I dunno. I'm not a brother but I do know some individuals who are. They're thoroughly decent people apparently using the network for the right reasons. Is there any truth in the tales of what goes on in the upper reaches of the hierarchy – and if so, are these guys aware of it?

Only they can tell us – but the very nature of their organization, doing most of its business and carrying out the bulk of its practices behind closed doors – means they can't.

They are bound by that bond of secrecy and loyalty – and strictly forbidden to break it through fear of consequences if they do. How serious those repercussions would be is shrouded in mystery, therefore wide open to wild speculation and dire forebodings.

Many world leaders have been Freemasons, including US presidents, British Prime Ministers and members of our Royal family.

The Knights of Malta, the Golden Dawn, the Catholic Church's Opus Dei and the notorious Skull and Bones Society in America are other secretive groups often cited as part of the global elite/Illuminati network placing folk in power and controlling them.

The ultimate aim is a single government, army and religion – the New World Order.

Other bodies working to this end are often said to be the highly influential Trilateral Commission (USA, Europe, and Japan), the Royal Institute of International Affairs, the Round Table, Committee of 300, Bilderberg Group and the Tavistock Institute.

They are allegedly full of current world leaders and those of the recent past, still very active.

Like robbers dividing up their haul, they sometimes quarrel, fall out and work against each other.

But they have the same selfish zeal to run the world for their own benefit, hoarding all the wealth and power at the expense of everyone else, seeing us as their slaves to be viciously exploited.

August 13 – Wow! – Team GB is up to third in the Rio medals table with 22, seven of them gold. The USA still leads with 50 medals while China has 37.

Gold-grabbing cyclist Sir Bradley Wiggins became the first Briton to win eight Olympic medals as our athletes achieved three gold and three silver on day seven yesterday.

Rowers Heather Stanning and Helen Glover won the pairs, repeating their gold medal success at the London Olympics four years ago. We also clinched the men's fours. The silvers came in dressage, trampolining and swimming.

August 14 – Mo Farah and Laura Trott both made history by each claiming their third Olympic titles as Great Britain won eight more medals in Rio, staying third in the table.

Jess Ennis-Hill took silver in the heptathlon – a gruelling seven-event contest taking in running, jumping shot put and javelin – and long jumper Greg Rutherford clinched bronze.

Mo overcame a tumble to win the 10,000 metres, while Laura's women's pursuit cycling team beat the USA with a world record.

The men's eight rowers won gold while the women came second. Other silver medals came in swimming and cycling.

American swimming legend Michael Phelps bowed out of the Olympics with a record 23rd career gold as Team GB came second in the men's four by 100 metres relay.

Yesterday was also a triumph at my beloved Bell, where a family fun day in aid of Julia's House children's hospices was a resounding success in the bright sunshine.

My friend Martine Phillips-Hannen – my great buddy Jem's daughter – helped host the event, which attracted a huge number of familiar, friendly faces including Sarah Garbutt, Paul Dangerfield and their seven kids. I gave them spare, signed paperback copies of my books.

It was the third charity event Laura, Mark, Nicola and co had laid on this year. All three have luckily been blessed with good weather – so crucial to success with heavy use of the garden.

August 14, seven hours later – Just got back from a lovely time down the beach in the blazing sunshine with Phil, Emily and Chloe. Fabulous!

August 15 – Topped off yesterday excellently with another great evening session at the Bell in the company of Paul and Sarah, Penny, Mark Hemington, John Gaynor, John Palmer, Matt Brant, Lou Delahaye and her feller Brian, DJ Ross, Darren and guv'nors Laura and Mark.

In Rio, Scottish tennis player Andy Murray won his second consecutive Olympic gold as Team GB rose to second in the medals table yesterday.

Murray retained the men's singles title he won at the London Olympics four years ago to grab our 15th gold of the Brazilian games.

Max Whitlock grabbed two of them in the gymnastics arena and Justin Rose triumphed on the golf course, while cyclist Jason Kenny – Laura Trott's feller – beat team-mate Callum Skinner into second place to claim his fifth Olympic gold.

This takes him level in the all-time golden greats stakes with fellow cyclist Sir Bradley Wiggins and rower Sir Steve Redgrave, also each with five, one behind Sir Chris Hoy's six.

Wiggins remains the most decorated British Olympian ever with eight medals in all.

Also yesterday, Jamaica's Usain Bolt achieved his record third Olympics 100 metres title.

Team GB's haul of 15 medals in 24 hours – including those five glittering gold ones – means now being placed second to the USA, which has 69 in all, 26 of them gold.

Our lads and lasses have now leapfrogged China, which has more medals in total (45 to GB's 38) but only 13 silvers to our team's 16). Both squads have 15 gold.

But – oh dear! – AFC Bournemouth went down 3-1 at home to Manchester United in the first weekend of the new Premier League season.

This means that, after just one game played, United are top of the table and the Cherries are rock bottom. But it's very early days yet, right?

Leaving sport for general news, four people died and thousands had to be rescued after heavy rains brought widespread flooding in Louisiana, USA.

And 16 died and 200 were injured as violence rocked Kashmir following the killing of a popular separatist leader. The region is a flashpoint zone between India, Pakistan and China.

August 16 – I've just been for another saunter through Fisherman's Walk to the cliff top but the grass had just been cut so there were lots of flying insects about, so I decided to retreat and sit by the pond at the entrance to the wooded area instead. The hot sun beamed down.

While there, I saw my friend Sam Lowney walking her two dogs before she started a work shift at Southbourne's Brewhouse and Kitchen restaurant/bar, formerly the Malt and Hops and before that, the Pinecliff – my first local on moving to Bournemouth in the late 1970s.

Earlier this year, Sam switched to the Brewhouse from the Bell, where she had been bar manager. Her pal and mine Nicola Williams, then her deputy, took over when she left.

Another gold medal and four more silvers have kept Great Britain in second place in Rio.

Londoner Charlotte Dujardin won the individual dressage – the first British woman to retain an individual gold at any Olympic Games.

Mark Cavendish, 31, finally bagged an Olympic medal, coming second in the men's omnium cycle event in controversial style after causing a crash that almost took out his main rival Elia Viviani. Fortunately, the Italian regained his composure and made up ground to take the gold.

Three other silvers were added to our overall tally and Burnley's Sophie Hitchon took bronze in the hammer, the first GB female to do so.

August 17 – Laura Trott and Jason Kenny are Britain's new golden couple after a sensational day for our record-smashing team in Rio.

Essex girl Laura, aged 24, became GB's most successful female Olympian ever by winning the omnium cycling contest. It was her second gold in Brazil and her fourth altogether.

Fiancé and fellow cyclist Jason, 28, from Bolton, equalled Sir Chris Hoy's six gold with victory in the keirin. Laura and Jason are due to marry next month.

Sailor Giles Scott also grabbed gold and there were silver medals for divers Jack Laugher and cyclist Becky James. Bronzes came in cycling, boxing and gymnastics, where we gained two.

The nine medals clinched by Britain on day 11 gives them two more than at the same stage during London 2012 – to date Team GB's most successful games ever.

Our 50 medals in all – 19 of them gold – keep us second to the USA with a total of 84.

August 18 – It was Bell barman Mikey Delahaye's 21st birthday yesterday, so last night a whole host of us turned up at the pub for a surprise party. It was brill and he was blown away.

There's an item on today's news about a sharp and shocking rise in Islamophobic attacks – physical, verbal and through social media sites. And they always increase significantly just after terrorist incidents at home or abroad.

While shocking this is hardly surprising, given the tendency of some folk to believe all the blatant and frequent anti-Muslim Press reports and blame Islamists for everything, and the strong feelings of suspicion – hatred even – many have of those of a different faith or race.

I detest prejudice based on sexual, religious or ethnic concerns, which I find both ignorant and actually rather silly, given my Oneness worldview. So this fresh surge in anti-Muslim violence and insults appals me.

I'm both saddened and alarmed that folk can so easily fall into the divide and rule trap set by our dark overlords via their Parliamentary and media lackeys. This evil and corrosive tactic, keeping them firmly in control and us fighting each other instead of them, is working a treat.

August 19 – It's been a family affair for Team GB at Rio with the Brownlee brothers taking gold and silver in the triathlon, a three-sport event involving swimming, cycling and running.

Alistair Brownlee, 28, retained the Olympic gold he won four years ago in London while sibling Jonny, 26, came second; improving on the bronze medal he took in 2012.

The Yorkshire duo's success yesterday was headline news as our lads and lasses brought another flurry of glittering discs to stay second with 56 medals, 22 of them gold.

Welsh-born Jade Jones, 23, retained the taekwondo title she won at the London Olympics.

The USA remains top with 100, including 35 gold, while China stays third with two more in total but two fewer gold and five fewer silver.

August 20 – Had another booze and fun session at Sam and Carl's yesterday evening with them, Rudy, Bailey, Tina Mcauley, Jem Hannen, the dogs Albert and Bramble – and our friend Kelly Millen, back in town for her son Ryan's birthday next week.

It was great to see Kelly again. She's lived in Doncaster or the past couple of years but is talking about moving back to Pokesdown, where her daughter Jade also still lives in a flat share with Ryan.

In Rio, Nick Skelton has proved that the old ones are the best by winning gold for Team GB at the age of 58. Okay, I say old even though he's four years my junior. But in sporting terms it is regarded as an astonishing age to be a world beater – especially given his history.

Veteran show jumper Skelton, taking part in his seventh Games, is the oldest medallist in Rio and the oldest ever in Olympic equestrian history. He won the individual event yesterday on 13-year-old bay stallion Big Star.

Warwickshire-born Skelton initially retired 16 years ago after breaking his neck in two places, but fought back to fitness to collect gold in the London 2012 team event. He's also had a hip replaced and is a long-time sufferer with back pain. Now that's what I call a hero!

Equally brilliant Big Star is the horse equivalent – also returning to show jumping's biggest stage following injuries that have beset him since the pair's London Games triumph.

Our women's hockey team beat hot favourites the Netherlands in a dramatic penalty shoot out – clinching Great Britain's first ever gold in the event and dethroning the winners of both the Beijing 2008 and London 2012 tournaments.

World champions the Dutch are the most successful team in women's hockey history.

These two more gold, a silver and a bronze keeps Team GB second with 24 gold, 60 in all.

Runner Usain Bolt, 29, brought his outstanding Olympic career to a spectacular close, completing world-beating "triple triple" by leading Jamaica to victory in the men's four by 100 metres relay.

The world's fastest man received his ninth gold with a clean sweep of the 100 metres, 200 metres and sprint relay in the last three Games tournaments. He's now retiring on top.

You may have noticed that I've wittered on about the Olympics but not much else in my journal entries of the past few days. That's because our athletes are doing so amazingly well and it does seem to be otherwise the usual August news silly season with not a lot happening.

August 21 – Talk about tempting fate! Fifty people have been killed and nearly 100 wounded in an alleged bomb attack on a Kurdish wedding in Gaziantep, Turkey.

No-one has yet claimed responsibility but it's suspected the dreaded Islamic State was behind the explosion, close to the Syrian border in an area said to have several IS cells.

A suicide bomber is thought to have targeted the wedding guests as they danced in the street.

At the Olympics, Mo Farah successfully defended his 5,000 metre title to claim gold as Team GB pushed our medal total to 66 – one better than at London 2012 with still a day to go.

The excellent London performance was itself Britain's best medal haul for over 100 years.

Wins for boxer Nicola Adams and canoeist Liam Heath helped take GB's gold tally to 27 as our athletes won another six medals yesterday.

Adams successfully defended her flyweight title won at London while Heath won the kayak single 200 metres sprint. With 22 silver and 17 bronze now, this keeps us second to the USA.

I mentioned most of our gold medallists as the Games story unfolded but I missed a few. So, in the spirit of fairness, here they are: sailors Hannah Mills and Saskia Clark, rower Phelan Hill and kayaker Joe Clarke.

And I guess I should also stress that Bradley Wiggins' eighth Olympic gold came in the men's pursuit cycling, where he was part of a four-member team setting a new world record.

Turning to my hectic social life (ha ha!), I had a good time at the Bell last night with Kelly Millen, her daughter Jade and son Ryan – having a few early birthday drinks. Sam's son Alex Hall, a very close friend of all of them, was also there.

So was John Gaynor, Krissie Benbow, Paul Clyde, a pleasant Dutch feller called Guus, a regular called Darren and a mate of mine called Jim (don't know their surnames). Tony Jeffery and Lottie Wragg served us our drinks while guv'nors Mark and Laura mingled.

August 22 – It's now thought that the Turkey suicide bomber was between 12 and 14 years old. Many of the victims were children too. Good grief!

Londoner Joe Joyce, 30, picked up silver in the super heavyweight boxing to take our final Rio tally to 67 – the best result ever on away soil – on the last day of the sporting spectacular.

Third-placed China actually clinched three more discs overall, but our athletes grabbed one more gold and five more silvers than theirs to keep second place behind the USA, which finished with 121 total, 46 of them gold.

By all account, the Rio Olympics were a triumph. But please let's not forget the alarming backdrop – a country where some are very wealthy but millions live in poverty as inequality reigns and lawlessness, brutal authoritarianism and widespread human rights abuses are rife.

August 23 – I was watching a You Tube programme last night and it contained the quote "War is when your government tells you who the enemy is. A revolution is when you figure it out yourself" – attributed to Anonymous.

I like that. Okay, granted it's a bit simplistic and I would never support a violent overthrow of any kind, but it's a quite neat though cynical way of summarizing a far too familiar situation.

****

CHAPTER SEVEN

Friends Reunited

August 24 – Had another very pleasant, quiet, chilled Tuesday afternoon session at the Bell yesterday with Laura, Mark, Nicola, Alex, Darren and adorable pub puppy Flick, who sat on a chair next to me and promptly fell asleep, bless her!

Speaking of the Bell, it's been marvellous seeing my very good friends Paul Dangerfield and Sarah Garbutt again back at their old watering hole. Where they belong, many of us say.

The fortnight plus they've been here holidaying from Wexford, Ireland – their home of a dozen years – has intensified Paul's determination to move back here as soon as possible.

They went because they didn't want to bring up their children in Boscombe, but those kids are older now and all thoroughly enjoyed visiting this area, where their grandparents still live.

Sarah and Paul's daughter Rosie brought her Irish boyfriend Sean – a pleasant lad on his first holiday out of his native country.

Just to explain, Paul is actually from Manchester but, like me, has spent most of his life in Bournemouth and similarly treats it very much as his home town.

Another pal who wants to move back is Kelly Millen, who relocated to Doncaster about three years ago due to problems locally. Her son Ryan and daughter Jade share a flat close to here.

It was great to catch Kelly again at the weekend and an added bonus was seeing our mutual friend Roz Tidiman, a really close mate of both Paul and Sarah, who treat her like a sister.

Roz has given up the booze and can now happily sit in a pub drinking coffee or fruit juice without being tempted – while her friends get tipsy or sozzled. She finds us very amusing.

Turning to today's news, a magnitude 6.2 earthquake has struck central Italy, killing at least 21 people and leaving many others trapped under rubble. Terrible!

August 25 – The death toll has reached 247 as emergency services dig beneath the debris.

Meanwhile, five people are known to have died at Camber Sands, Sussex, on the hottest day of the year yesterday. A search for a sixth person spotted in the sea will resume today.

Three men died after being pulled from the water and two bodies were discovered nearby later. Local police say there's nothing to suggest the dead were migrants, a very strange comment to make – unless there's a good chance that they actually were.

I, for one, wouldn't have even considered that possibility unless the coppers had planted the idea in my mind.

There's a lot of talk on the news about bids to gag hate-mongering extremists on the Internet. This is nuts because the attention it's giving them is actually providing the vital publicity they need and thrive on. Ignore, marginalize and isolate them and rob them of their power I say!

Just as with street corner zealots, we may detest their radical rabble rousing with a passion. But we must also firmly defend their right to freedom of speech and expression – even if what they're saying is ugly, toxic and bitterly divisive, upsetting and angering us.

Because you can't have that basic human right for some people and not for others, based totally on your own blatant bias towards the ones saying things you like and against those voicing opinions you don't. That's infantile – a dangerous perversion of a golden principle.

One of the main reasons given for silencing the hate-peddlers is that they can coax others into taking up arms – using bombs, bullets and knives to wreak murder and mayhem.

Well one, this is a very subjective matter indeed and the comment could be applied to many scenarios. I think of the Kitchener poster "your country needs you" and Churchill's "we'll fight them on the beaches" speech. Each incited violence. Right motives but lethal outcomes?

Two, if people are that mentally fragile and easily led they're probably going to get into serious trouble anyway without any help from deranged crazies spouting poisonous bile.

And three, to state the obvious, it will be these unhinged whack jobs unleashing any deadly devastation – not the obnoxious individuals uttering hate-fuelled rhetoric from the sidelines.

That's the favourite tactic of community leaders of all kinds who follow set agendas, using their powers of persuasion to get others to fight their battles while they themselves stay safe.

So I advise letting the tunnel-vision unstable extremists have their say. Just don't listen to them. And certainly avoid being conned into doing their dirty work for them. That's insane!

At the end of the day, either you believe in freedom of expression or you don't. You can't pick and choose. And the rights, wrongs and morality of fierce words and their consequences all depend on where you stand – which side of any political, religious or ideological divides.

August 26 – Happy birthday Claire Kimber, my old pal from those halcyon days at the Bell going back over 20 years or so.

She was the bar manager and a key member of that whole close community comprising Kerry, Theresa, Paula, Jem, Paul and Sarah, Debs and Al, Paul Moran, John Gaynor, Steve Elvidge, John Palmer and others.

Two items on the RT telly news this morning concerned me and set me thinking. One was about a car bomb exploding at a police headquarters in Turkey, killing 11 and injuring 78.

Dangerously unstable Turkey, currently being ripped apart by civil war, is a very important country indeed, standing as it does at the crossroads of the world, both geographically and culturally. Anything happening there is bound to resonate across the globe.

Another land ravaged by a bitter and bloody civil war is Syria, where it's estimated that half a million people have died in conflict over the past five years. Today's RT report centred on the shocking use of chemical weapons that have apparently caused many of these deaths.

Hundreds of thousands of refugees have fled, mostly to Europe, as other countries have intervened, some using military might, to apparently try to sort out the problems.

I say apparently, because many cynics would claim that these other nations just want to protect their own interests while making a fast buck from all the turmoil and misery.

Because, just like Turkey, Syria is a country of great significance and interest to other nations including the USA, Britain, Russia and France – due to its strategic location at the heart of the volatile Middle East.

Consequently, RT, the BBC, Sky, other news channels and the daily papers frequently cover unfolding events in these crucial territories.

There's a lot less coverage of the crisis in Venezuela, South America, where there's been a total collapse of the economy following a plummet in the price of oil, its most vital export.

Civil unrest, crime and corruption are rife as shops stand empty and fears grow of a violent bloodbath followed by a fierce crackdown.

So what is the answer to all these crises? What can we do to help the huge numbers of our fellow human beings suffering and dying in these troubled lands? It is heartbreaking.

I dunno, but I do vehemently believe that sending in troops and bombers isn't the way and only acerbates the problems. If a foreign government is killing and brutalizing its people we should certainly step in to try and stop it. But how?

That's the million dollar question and it's not an easy one to answer. Diplomatic pressure, arm-twisting, threats of boycotts, economic sanctions, withdrawal of financial help and refusal to sell weapons might be starting points – with military intervention as a last resort.

But then we need to ask ourselves – how would we feel if another nation decided to similarly actively intervene in our own domestic affairs? We'd tell them to sling their hooks!

Okay, I accept that we'd want someone to rescue us if we were being in any way mistreated. But from abroad, thousands of miles away? No, from a lot closer to home I'd suggest.

I'm very tempted here to facetiously point out that in fact our own coalition government, and then the later Tory administration, did indeed seriously abuse and bully ill, disabled and frail people in its care and should have been brought to book for these disgraceful acts of cruelty.

It's even arguable that savage policies led to financial ruin and premature deaths for many unfortunates in our land. But I'm not claiming for one moment that the severity or scale of atrocities was anywhere near as extreme as those taking place in Syria, Turkey or Venezuela.

I'm just saying that those being brutalized and exploited deserve to be helped, wherever they are on Earth. And our own political leaders should have expected criticism from abroad. But there's a world of difference between making your disgust known and invading foreign soil.

August 27 –It's now known that three Brits were among almost 300 people killed by that earthquake in Italy, where today's been designated as a national day of mourning.

Meanwhile, Russia and the USA are holding talks in a bid to establish a ceasefire as the first step towards a peaceful solution to the Syrian crisis, where both countries have used bombing campaigns in support of rival groups in the blood soaked civil war.

August 29 – Another Middle Eastern land being wracked by civil war is Yemen, where at least 45 people were yesterday killed by a suicide bomber driving a car into a wall at a military compound in the port city of Aden.

More than 6,000 have died since a rebel group called the Houthi seized control last January. Yemen is another key country strategically positioned at the crossroads of Africa and Asia.

But over in South America, six decades of civil have ended in Colombia with the leftist rebel group Farc announcing a ceasefire between itself and the government.

I find it interesting but very worrying that so many Middle Eastern, African, Asian and South American nations are or have been blighted by brutal dictatorships, extremes of wealth and poverty, corruption and sustained lethal fighting. Chile, Nigeria and Brazil spring to mind.

It's Bank Holiday Monday and I've had a good weekend. Saturday I went to Sam's to see her, Carl, Rudy, Bailey, our friend Tina and the family dogs Albert and Bramble. And last night I was at the Bell for karaoke final night.

My good buddy Jem won the contest with a rousing version of Minnie the Moocher. Other friends present included Mark Hemington, Penny and Dawn, Matt Brant, Mikey Delahaye, John Gaynor, Sarah Spence, Paul Clyde, Sam Lowney and a new friend called Sue Seeney.

August 29, seven hours later – Just back from a wonderful time with Chloe, Harvey, Emily and Phil at Southbourne's sun-scorched beach followed by a meal at the cliff top Commodore Hotel. I had a tasty leek, spud mash and spring onion pie with baby potatoes, same as Emily.

August 30 – Happy 52nd birthday to my great pal Jem Hannen. Hope you have a good day, sausage!

But Jem will be as saddened as I am to learn of the demise of Hollywood actor Gene Wilder at the age of 83 after complications brought on by Alzheimer's disease.

Wilder is probably best known for his leading role in the classic family film *Willy Wonka and the Chocolate Factory*, based on Roald Dahl's children's book. But Jem and I loved him in the superb Mel Brooks comedies *Blazing Saddles*, *Young Frankenstein* and the *Producers*.

August 30, 4pm – Just spent a lovely afternoon in the Bell beer garden for my four-weekly catch up, booze and laughs session with Paula Carruthers – also involving Nicola Williams, Mark Evans, Laura Williams, Krissie Benbow, Paul Clyde, Steve and adorable pub dog Flick.

September 1 – My good mate Paul Dangerfield, referred to a few times already in this book, is 50 today. Have a blinding golden anniversary buddy!

September 3 – Remembering my mate Andy Frend, who passed on a year ago today. I've lit a candle for him and I put a little tribute on Facebook earlier.

It's Boscombe Community Fair weekend so yesterday evening I braved the overcast skies and drizzle to pop along to King's Park for the music and fun event raising money for local projects benefiting local people. I wasn't disappointed.

I met my good pals Jeff and Tina McNally there – they were helping man the Homes for Heroes stall with our mutual friend Paul Clyde, a fellow Bell regular.

Homes for Heroes is the charity that helps ex-services personnel sleeping rough. Paul, Tina and Jeff are with the local outreach team that provides food, clothing and practical assistance to these disgracefully abandoned veterans.

I bought a snazzy hat from a lovely lady called Gina, who gave me some incense sticks as we chatted for ages about music at her hippie accessories stall as she awaited customers. Sweet!

And, as always, the music was a key component in this mini-festival gathering of the clans. I left before headline act Dubheart did their set but I was lucky enough to be at the fair early enough to catch their impressive sound check.

I do love this local dub reggae act that recently appeared on telly for reaching the finals of a BBC best part-time band competition. I've got their album Mental Slavery and it's excellent.

Dubheart performed on the main stage while other musicians and poets displayed their talents in a tent offering food, a place to sit out of the rain and live entertainment.

One of the artists here was a very talented teenaged singer-songwriter called Nicole, accompanying herself on ukulele and guitar as she did her own songs and some great covers.

When I told Jeff about this he beamed: "That's my niece!" and promptly took me to meet her. I bought her four-track CD of self-penned material, which I'm playing now. It's superb.

A star of the future? I certainly hope so; remember the name – Nicole McNally. And remember where you heard it first!

I also enjoyed the groups Dreamcatcher and Hello Hawaii, both very good.

I love the community fair. As I've said before, this is my kind of event with my kind of people.

September 4 – Attitude can be okay – cool even – if backed up by talent or wisdom. But far too often it's just irritating crap.

Hundreds of mourners have this morning gathered for the funerals of the five young men who died after getting into difficulty in the sea at Camber Sands.

It's now known that the dead were all from London and very much part of their local community there – not migrants at all.

The only suggestion they might have been came just after the tragedy when Sussex police issued a bizarre denial that they were – a seemingly implausible notion up to that point.

I find it sinister and worrying that the bogey word "migrant" is so carelessly bandied about in these unsettling times of increasing ethnic friction.

Our thoughts are with the families of the unfortunate five.

Pope Francis has proclaimed the late Mother Teresa a saint for her sterling work helping India's poor and starving.

Tens of thousands have flocked to St Peter's Square, the Vatican, for the mass and canonisation today.

Mother Teresa, who died in 1997, had her critics – especially of her hard line Roman Catholic stance – but is generally regarded as one of the 20th century's good guys.

September 5 – Returned to Boscombe Community Fair yesterday and spent an excellent afternoon soaking up more good friendly vibes, more brilliant poetry, a hilariously chaotic dog show and more supremely succulent music.

I loved the Bonsai Pirates, Mischa and his Merry Men and the Daisie Ukuladies, four women giving an intriguing and highly entertaining ukulele-based twist on a Meghan Trainor song and some 1980s pop classics. Quite wonderful!

I chatted to Paul Clyde again and also my new friend Gina, who I bought some incense sticks from. She blew me a kiss as I waved goodbye on leaving the event.

And I had a brief conversation with my good pal Jaymi Darragh, who was helping serve booze at the fair's bar. Nice!

In fact, it's been a nice weekend all round in which I also saw Mark Hemington, Nicola Williams, Mark Chastney, Sarah and Darren Spence, Louise Delahaye, Laura Williams, Mark Evans, Tony Jeffery, Ross Maslin, John Gaynor and Jim – still don't know his surname.

September 6 – Heard some very bad news last night – my cousin Sandra has passed away. So yet another family member has been taken by cancer, meaning I'll be off once again soon to Bournemouth Crematorium, where I've said goodbye to far too many relatives and friends.

It's said you know you're getting old when you're attending more funerals than weddings – a rather witty way of reflecting a stark sad truth. But this is beyond a joke now – way beyond.

September 7 – Happy birthday to my niece Lisa, who's in her forties now, and also to Lottie, two today – daughter of my nephew Scott, therefore Lisa's own niece. Hope both have a ball.

As for myself, I had another pleasant afternoon in the Bell yesterday with Laura and Mark, Nicola and her Mark, a nice chap called Steve and his mate Phil, who took along a cute little terrier dog he was looking after for his chiropodist while she was away on holiday.

September 8 – Joyous tidings! – *Sunshine and Ice Volumes 10 (Glittering Stars), 11 (Amazing Messages)* and *12 (Humour and Miracles)* are now available through Amazon/Kindle, Waterstones, Bookfinder, Abe Books and others.

They cover the period from December 2014 to May 2016.

Volumes One to Nine are also still available and apparently you can get hold of my paperbacks in the UK, Ireland, Germany, the USA and Australia. Of 47 booksellers rating them, 42 have given a five star rating, with the other five giving four stars. Cool!

I'm again listening to Dubheart's Mental Slavery album and in the last few days I've enjoyed my new CDs by the Bonsai Pirates, Nicole McNally and Mischa and his Merry Men, plus Keane, the Levellers, Inspiral Carpets, two collections of early Beatles stuff and a compilation of 1960s number ones.

On the eating and drinking front, I've been increasing my consumption of healthy stuff such as green tea, unsalted nuts, salmon as well as tuna and oats and bran in addition to my usual breakfast cereals made of wheat, corn and rice.

I'm switching to cooking with virgin olive oil and will have dark chocolate as a rare treat.

I've also tried the bacon-style no-meat high-protein rashers made by Quorn – alongside their sausages, mince, chicken-style burgers and cottage pies. Delicious!

For the rest, its fruit juices, wholemeal bread, vegetables, thin-sliced ham and chicken, skimmed milk, half-fat bacon, garlic granules rather than white salt, Ryvita, Flora light margarine, items low in fat, sugar and salt and primarily white meat with red occasionally.

On average I have between one and four of the recommended five a day – on a good day it's five and on a bad day, none – and I try – but don't always succeed – to keep my alcohol consumption within 21 units per week.

Speaking of which, while I was in the pub the other day, landlady Laura returned from the dentists. The conversation that followed reminded me of an experience I had many moons ago when I was about 17.

I needed to have a bridge built in the lower front part of my mouth, involving filing two teeth down to points and then jamming three non-removable falsies in – the two outside ones hollow to fit over the points and the middle one filling in a gap where a tooth hadn't grown.

The dentist gave me an injection and went off for about ten minutes, returning to start work. But I could feel what he was doing so he had to stop to give me another jab. He tried again with the same result, so gave me two further injections before finally doing the necessary.

But I could still feel it, though not as much, and was in some pain as he carried out the procedure. He was mystified, saying most people only needed one jab of anaesthetic and I had enough in my jaw to "kill the mouth of a bull elephant."

Leaving the surgery, I boarded a bus to go home – just as the painkiller finally kicked in. It was so embarrassing. The driver thought I was drunk or brain-damaged as I tried with some difficulty to articulate where I wanted to go while dribbling uncontrollably!

For many years after that I had to be put under a general anaesthetic at hospital whenever I underwent serious dental work – fortunately only once, when a broken stub had to come out after the Christmas 2001 assault detailed in *Volume Two (Descent Into Darkness)*.

I think the modern anaesthetics must be much better because I've had root canal work and a filling in more recent times and my dentist managed to do both without me feeling a thing.

September 9 – The Rio de Janeiro Paralympics have started with Team GB netting seven medals, four gold, on the opening day – putting them second to China with 11 medals.

Dame Sarah Storey, 38, became Britain's most successful female Paralympian ever by clinching a career 12th gold medal. She did it by winning the C5, 3,000 metre individual pursuit cycling final. Fellow Briton Crystal Lane got the silver.

Steve Bate and Megan Giglia also picked up cycling gold and our fourth went to swimmer Ollie Hynd.

Last night I watched again that excellent film *Sliding Doors*, bought on DVD for £1.50p in a Southbourne charity shop the other day.

For any that don't know, it's a cleverly constructed, wittily written, wonderfully cut and well acted story of how the simple slip of missing a train can transform someone's fortunes.

It makes you so well aware of the huge impacts that fate, chance encounters and split-second timing can have on your life. I love movies like this that make you think.

The 1998 film is a romantic comedy written and directed by Peter Howitt with a strong cast headed by Gwyneth Paltrow and John Hannah.

Been playing Led Zeppelin One, Lynyrd Skynyrd's Greatest Hits and an album of Aerosmith's best cuts being performed live.

September 10 – Had a great time yesterday afternoon and early evening with Sam Excell, Carl Young, their family, pets and several friends. Cool!

Meanwhile, Team GB picked up seven more gold medals in Rio, pushing their total to 27 and keeping them second in the table to China.

Russia and the USA have agreed terms of a ceasefire in Syria as they jointly try to find a solution to that country's problems.

Whoop whoop! – AFC Bournemouth have won their first game of the season to climb to 14th in the Premier League table with four points from as many matches. They beat West Brom 1-0 at home after previously drawing with Crystal Palace and losing to Man U and West Ham.

****

CHAPTER EIGHT

Anniversaries

September 11 – Today's the 15th anniversary of the worst atrocity in modern times as crazed nutters ploughed planes into New York's twin towers and the Pentagon.

I've lit a candle for the victims and put a little tribute on Facebook.

And it's a year since Paula and I first shared a bed following our happy reunion. I recently ribbed her that we saw each other face to face for the first time in many years on July 7, 2015, 10th anniversary of the London Bombs, and got truly reunited exactly 14 years after 911.

I asked if these were pure coincidences or signs that our six-month relationship was doomed.

I'm not sure how pleased she was at the parallels I drew between key dates in our loving liaison and two huge global disasters but she did smile – or was it more of a grimace?

Yesterday evening I had a good time in the Bell with impressive rock covers band Fired Up and too many mates to mention. But I guess that's the point – Laura, Mark, Nicola and crew have attracted a whole legion of lovely people who all really get on.

It's how a local pub should be – and it's so flipping cool!

When I was round Sam's on Friday, she gave me a CD album by country rock star Melissa Etheridge to borrow and listen to. I've got it on now and it's very good. Guitarist and vocalist Melissa is an impressive performer and songwriter who comes up with some great lyrics.

September 11, 7pm – Went to a fun day and dog show at the Bell this afternoon, organized to raise money for the People's Dispensary for Sick Animals. Saw several mates there.

As the dog show bit started, I thought surely they should be emphasizing the rules – no biting or scratching through fear of disqualification. And the same should apply to the pets.

And watching the mayhem unfold, I facetiously came up with three new categories for the competition – loudest, fattest and stupidest in show – with similar categories for the dogs.

September 12 – A brand new lyric has assembled itself in my befuddled brain. Here it is:

Slipping on a CD, sipping at my green tea, lazing in my cosy chair
Walking through a woodland, talking of a good stand, puzzled
*   people stop and stare*
Shaking off reduced wealth, making plans for rude health, trying
*   hard to raise some smiles*
Living in the bus lane, giving in to just plain tiredness from clocked
*   up miles*

Settling in a warm rut, getting over deep cut, wonder what the
*   future holds*
Will I suit a sweetheart? Contribute to fine art? Find a sparkler in
*   the folds?*
Am I making sense guys? Bad mistake or quite wise? Am I being
*   just like me?*
Facing facts and old age, racing to the last page, this is how it
*   seems to be.*

Living through these dusky days,
Strolling though this misty haze
Taking things so smooth and steadily
Steering clear of hate and mess
Sick to death of strife and stress
Family and friends are all to me.

Speeding times are not good, feeding minds like I should – better
*   say that's what I try to do*

Spending days with good sound, spreading light rays all round,
*   making it ok for me and you*
This is now my life plan, helping while I still can, easing pain and
*   sadness that I find*
Had my share of trouble, bad despair twice double, aiming for
*   some peace of mind*

Living through these dusky days,
Strolling though this misty haze
Taking things so smooth and steadily
Steering clear of hate and mess
Sick to death of strife and stress
Family and friends are all to me.

'Dusky Days', Martin Money
September 10–12, 2016

September 14 – It's a Wednesday and I've had a great start to my week – NOT! Monday I endured a dental appointment and yesterday I attended a family funeral.

I know no-one in their right mind enjoys seeing their dentist – unless they're also a loved one of course – but, as previously explained, for me it's a right ordeal as I have to take an anti-biotic solution beforehand through fear of a mouth infection making a beeline for my heart.

It applies even for my six-monthly check up and clean, which this was – for any blood drawn could prove fatal. Thank goodness it's all over now and I'm apparently okay. I dread going.

The funeral, at Bournemouth Crematorium, was my cousin Sandra's. It meant yet another visit to that wretched place to say farewell to a loved one. I'm sick of it!

My "adopted sister" Suzette took me in her car and we met Carol, David and other relatives at the funeral and then went to the wake at the Southbourne home that Sandra – Sandy – had shared with Alan, her partner of 26 years who she married in May while undergoing treatment following her cancer diagnosis.

(She actually died of a stroke on September 4 but it was obviously brought on by her failing health. Alan asked for donations to be sent to the stroke unit at the Royal Bournemouth Hospital, where Sandy died. I duly did so in addition to having bought a floral wreath.)

It was good to see my sis Carol and hubby David again and also our cousins Eric and Colin – Sandy's brothers – plus another cousin called Andrew, the guy who exchanged text messages with me when I was in hospital with my heart crisis (see *Vol 3 Pt 2, Scalpels and Angels*).

Suzette had to leave the wake early to go home and tend to her dog, Poppy, so we stayed just long enough to be polite and pay our respects before she dropped me off back here, my flat.

I changed my clothes and walked to the Bell for a drink in Sandy's memory. I knew she would have approved and, besides, it was a Tuesday, my normal afternoon for going there.

Oh, and there was a thunderstorm in the morning.

Also yesterday, my good friend Sam Excell went to hospital for more tests as they try to find out what's wrong after several recent health scares. Hope all went okay for her.

In a happier vein, it was our mutual mate Tina Mcauley's birthday. Wishing her all the best and trusting she had a good one.

On the music front I've been revisiting the delights of Big Country, the Traveling Wilburys, Echo and the Bunnymen, the Smiths and Pink.

Big Country's mighty Just a Shadow is one of those songs that gets me every time, inspiring me to do a passionate air guitar dance and even sing as it sends that vital shiver up and down my spine. Yes me, dance and sing – well, sort of, and only in the privacy of my own home.

Other tracks having the same affect on me include Soon by Yes, Plainsong by the Cure, While My Guitar Gently Weeps, Yes it Is,

It's Only Love, This Boy and The Long and Winding Road by the Beatles, Wild Horses by the Rolling Stones, Hairless Heart, Firth of Fifth and Many Too Many by Genesis, Badge by Cream and Persephone by Wishbone Ash.

Also this little lot – You Got Lucky (live) by Tom Petty, I Am Made of You by Alice Cooper, the Night Watch and Starless by King Crimson, Anthem by the Sensational Alex Harvey Band, Till the End by Motorhead, the Recollection by Rick Wakeman, Since I've Been Loving You (live) by Led Zeppelin and Jan Akkerman's guitar solo from Eruption by Focus.

Runaway by Hazel O'Connor, Still in Love with You by Thin Lizzy, Love Reign O'er Me by the Who, Man of the World and Freedom by Fleetwood Mac, Objects in the Rear View Mirror by Meat Loaf, Samba Pa Ti by Santana, Lost in the Flood by Bruce Springsteen, Still You Turn Me On by Emerson, Lake and Palmer and Whole of the Moon by the Waterboys.

Plus big chunks of the albums Marquee Moon (Television), Heaven and Hell (Black Sabbath), Close to the Edge (Yes) Aqualung (Jethro Tull) and Life's Rich Pageant (REM).

A lot of Pink Floyd and Mike Oldfield music also gives me that chilly but delicious thrill.

I'm naming just a few here off the top of my head to give you an idea of what floats my boat. The sensation is like having an orgasm with someone you're in love with. Yeah – that good!

September 16 – Happy birthday Roz Tidiman, hope you have a great one my friend. And half a year sober – good girl! we're all so proud of you!

At the Paralympics, our sportsmen and women are once again doing us proud, keeping us second in the medals table with 108 medals, 49 of them gold.

On the music front, I'm currently playing the album Mr Tambourine Man by the Byrds and yesterday I gave the Clash's marvellous London Calling long player another spin. I also dusted off a Cream compilation set.

And last night I thoroughly enjoyed some more intriguing, inspiring and ultimately pretty damned amazing items on You Tube through my telly.

One was a presentation put on by the late Wayne Dyer, an American psychologist, philosopher, author and motivational speaker who died last year aged 75.

He was a very wise man who came up with some great quotes, including these two used in his positive thinking piece I watched.

One was "change the way you look at things and the things you look at change", and the other, "loving people live in a loving world, hostile people live in a hostile world – same world."

Which are both great ways of saying that we create our own realities and they depend entirely on the way we view our lives and surroundings.

Some may consider such slick, smooth platitudes as rather twee – and a large part of me does too. We all know existence isn't non-stop sweetness and light. But I'm all for putting a positive spin on things where possible – not letting them bring us down or make us bitter.

Pain, tragedy, hatred, violence and negativity are unavoidable facts of life but we shouldn't let them control or define us. Shrug them off, laugh at them even – just don't give in to them.

But then, my sense of humour always does go into overdrive at sad, scary or stressful times – like at Sandy's funeral the other day, when I said to her brother Eric – "we really can't go on meeting like this" – which brought a poignant smile from him, as I knew it would.

I was referring to the fact that Eric and I had both also been at our mutual Auntie Joyce's funeral not all that long ago – June 2015 – our first face-to-face meeting in over 50 years.

Because that's the way our family's always been, using humour as a highly effective defence mechanism in circumstances where others would be shocked, viewing it as inappropriate and actually pretty flipping disrespectful.

Humour and the ability to find it in the most dark and depressing situations is so very important. Otherwise we'd crack up, go under or become nasty and resentful liabilities.

Speaking of great quotes, here's one of my favourites from iconic Indian good guy Mahatma Gandhi. Asked how he viewed Western civilisation, he said: "I think it would be a good idea." I think that's brilliant!

The intriguing aspect of You Tube last night was a mind-boggling two hour documentary claiming that the Earth was indeed actually flat – as believed centuries ago before we were allegedly fed an elaborate lie about it being a globe.

Not only that, there was a huge dome over it, meaning so-called space exploration and the moon landings were intricately-woven fantasies, no more real than Hollywood movies.

I know what you're thinking – this is crazy talk, hopelessly outdated and just plain backward and ignorant in these days of cutting edge technology and sophisticated ideas. I tend to agree.

But I still found the film fascinating, just as I do all the other absorbing but radically left field stuff I'm now finding on You Tube. It can be a lot more entertaining than mainstream TV!

And I always stand by my open minds argument, strongly advising caution in accepting or rejecting notions based purely on whether they're widely accepted or considered outlandish.

And, thinking about it, I can't see it making any difference to me whether the Earth is flat or round. We all have to live our own lives and deal with our immediate environs regardless of bigger pictures, wider perspectives or higher concepts. They just make for animated debates.

September 18 – It's Sunday morning and so far I've had a good weekend. Friday I sauntered up to Sam and Carl's for our customary weekly booze and silliness session that this time also involved Tina Mcauley and Jem Hannen.

Last night I made a last-minute decision to visit the Bell – and I'm so glad I did. Jem walked in about an hour after I did, asking if our pals Roz Tidiman, Paul Dangerfield and Sarah Garbutt had turned up yet. I didn't even know Sarah and Paul were back over from Ireland!

The couple duly appeared, and it was lovely to see them again so soon after their last visit. They had come over for a long weekend to celebrate with Paul's dad, 70 the other day, and their great pal and "adopted sister" Roz, whose birthday was Friday.

Roz arrived at the pub a bit later. Her brother was also there, along with John Gaynor, John Palmer, Billy Clarkson, Kelly Adams, Tim Robbins, Mark Thornton, Laura, Mark and others.

Tony Jeffery and Lottie Wragg served our drinks and live music was supplied by the rather impressive Permanent Vocation, doing rousing versions of Black Sabbath, Thin Lizzy, Deep Purple, Metallica, UFO and Ozzy Osbourne songs.

Meanwhile, in Rio de Janiero, our Paralympians have already surpassed their 2012 London medal haul as competitors enter into the last day of the Games. Team GB has 147 in all, 64 of them gold. Four years ago they amassed 120 total, 34 of them gold.

Their current tally keeps them second in the table to China with 237 medals including 105 gold. The Ukraine team sits third, with 117 in all, 41 of them gold.

Our lads and lasses have also risen a place – in London they came third behind China and Russia, not taking part this time around.

It's an amazing achievement all round – the best performance since the Seoul Paralympics in 188 when the Brits netted 183 medals including 65 gold.

Cyclist Sarah Storey picked up her third Rio gold, making a career total of 14, some of them in swimming. The Manchester 38-year-old is Britain's most decorated female Paralympian.

But the Rio Games have been tinged with sadness following the death yesterday of an Iranian cyclist who incurred head injuries then suffered a cardiac arrest after crashing on a mountain during a road race.

Meanwhile, in America, 29 people were hurt as an explosive device was detonated in the Chelsea area of New York as crowds enjoyed a Saturday night out. The exact details, motive and culprit or culprits have yet to be ascertained.

Been playing my CD of Slade's Greatest Hits – marvellous!

September 19 – Finished off the weekend with another visit to the Bell for the Sunday karaoke, in which my pals Jem Hannen, Mark Hemington and Nicola Williams took part.

Jem did a belting performance of Mustang Sally – his speciality – that brought the house down. Mark sang The Boxer and Your Song and Nic gave a fine rendition of I Will Survive.

Nicola, our lovely bar manager, also duetted with her feller Mark Chastney on Beautiful Liar and her mum Penny Williams on These Boots Are Made for Walking. Lots of fun!

Matt Brant, John Gaynor, Sarah and Darren Spence, Alex King and Demi Pitkin were also there and Lottie Wragg and a nice girl called Tasmin – Tas – were working behind the bar.

It was another super night at my local with several good friends, but we were all well aware that one of us was missing – Penny's great mate Dawn Lewis, stuck in hospital for tests after a suspected angina attack a few days ago. It was a shock to her and us and we wish her well.

In Rio, our lads and lasses did indeed finish second with 147 medals including 64 gold. China came top and the Ukraine, third. Very well done team, you did us proud again – and no doubt inspired a generation of young Paralympian hopefuls to keep up the good work. Excellent!

And on that very positive, life-affirming note, I shall end part one of this latest volume of *Sunshine and Ice*, a decidedly odd life journal. The rest follows at the turn of a page or two...

****

LAYERS OF PERCEPTION

Part Two

September to November 2016.

CHAPTER NINE

Melons And Collies

September 21 – Yesterday I went to the building society, took washing to the laundrette, had a haircut, picked up the washing and then paid my usual Tuesday afternoon visit to the Bell, seeing Ben, Nicola, Laura, Mark, Steve, Ian and barmaid Shannon. Good times!

Sitting in the barber's reminded me of an old joke from the seventies, a time when some young people grew their hair long and others had skinhead cuts. It went: "the youth of today are a melancholy lot – half look like melons and the other half resemble collies!" Ha ha!

Just playing Money for Nothing – the best of Dire Straits. Quality!

September 23 – Giant American internet information and communication company Yahoo is claiming that "state sponsored" hackers stole data from 500 million users in what appears to be the largest publicly disclosed cyber-breach in history.

What was I saying earlier in this book about being careful what sensitive details you pass on to other worldwide web users – and my fears about who has access and how they're used?

Swathes of personal information, including people's names, phone numbers, email addresses and "unencrypted security questions and answers", were hacked into in 2014 – but it's only just been made public. The FBI has confirmed it is investigating the alarming allegation.

I grudgingly accept that in these high-tech days when those bent on wreaking havoc have computers it's imperative that government security services can protect us all by fighting them on every front including the internet.

My concerns arise over cavalier definitions of the word "terrorist" and the levels of intrusion into the private lives of innocent people and surveillance, therefore control, this entails.

I'm now playing a bit of Eminem but earlier I enjoyed the aural delights of Metallica's brilliant trailblazing breakthrough album Master of Puppets, which took heavy metal into new areas – redefining it. I hadn't heard it for ages and had forgotten how bloody good it is.

I've also had Supertramp, Donovan and Rainbow on my CD player in the past two days.

September 24 – It's 12 noon on a Saturday here in sunny Bournemouth. And in Liverpool, Jeremy Corbyn has just been re-elected Labour leader at his party's autumn conference. The result and feedback are being broadcast live on telly as I type.

Corbyn racked up 61.8 per cent of the vote to beat challenger Owen Smith – a greater margin of victory than when he won the leadership contest just over a year ago with 59.5 per cent.

This is good news for our country for, as I've already stated more than once, left-winger Corbyn represents a fresh, genuine alternative to hard line, unjust and divisive Conservative policies – unlike the centre ground Labour MPs more interested in power than principles.

You know, the Tory wannabes – slippery, devious champagne socialists who act so like their elitist uncaring so-called rivals – dirty traitors too eager to betray Corbyn and knife his back.

For its these ambitious but unscrupulous Labour leading lights that have led the revolt against him – a seemingly decent guy with vision and integrity who's inspired a surge in party membership among voters sick of the Tory nightmare and craving a socialist response.

In a short conference speech immediately following the result announcement, Corbyn urged party members to put the arguments of the recent past behind them, unite to take on the Conservatives and win the next general election.

Speaking as a Green, I accept that my own party is unlikely to win power any time soon but I certainly welcome any move to oust the terrible Tories, especially if it's led by Corbyn.

Critics say he's unelectable and Smith would have a far better chance – but it would be a pointless exercise if a new centre-ground Labour government just carried on with tired old policies propping up the status quo with its own versions of unjust, inefficient conservatism.

We desperately need a new approach to politics and the running of our beloved country, not the same old same old that's created our current disastrous screw-up of a system.

That's why I'm a Green, and it's also why I'd back straight-talking, principled, clear-visioned Corbyn over callous, duplicitous, untrustworthy and traitorous so-called moderates any day.

It's about frigging time Labour stopped tearing itself apart and started to fight tooth and nail against our cruel overlords and the inequality, unfairness and misery infesting our fine land.

September 25 – Wishing a very happy birthday to my friend Penny Williams, who's on holiday abroad at the moment. I've just sent her a Facebook greeting.

September 26 – It's Monday and I've had a nice weekend. Saturday evening I went to the Bell and enjoyed the company of mates and rock and roll covers band Mellow Yellow. I felt so sorry for them – the pub was really quiet and they didn't get the support they deserved.

Had a lovely surprise yesterday – a visit from Phil, Emily, Chloe and Harvey. After coffee, kids' programmes and general mayhem at my flat, we adjourned to Fisherman's Walk, where the children terrorized the squirrels, and then the Commodore Hotel for a meal. Sweet!

Went to the pub again last night for another chilled karaoke session with DJ Ross Maslin, John Gaynor, John Palmer, Billy Clarkson, Matt Brant, Lottie Wragg, Tony Jeffery, Shannon Hanlon, Alex King, Demi Pitkin, Guus Bruin and the guv'nor Mark Evans. Cool!

(Laura was visiting her parents on the Isle of Wight.)

Ross told me he'd just heard that that an old boy called Harry, known to several regulars, had just died. I didn't know Harry, but he was clearly a much loved and respected guy. I felt especially sorry for birthday girl Penny, who was very close to him but temporarily away.

Turning to happier matters, I've just had a very pleasant encounter. I went to the One Stop shop up the road from here to be served by my friend Dawn Lewis – Penny's best mate – back at work after her recent suspected angina attack.

Dawn still has to have more tests but it was good to see her out of hospital and returned to circulation. I told her so and added that if she wanted to talk about heart issues I was available. She said thanks.

September 27, 4.30pm – Just had a splendid few hours at my beloved Bell with my exceedingly close pal Paula Carruthers, the very lovely bar manager Nicola Williams, guv'nor Mark Evans, Shannon "Smiler" Hanlon and others. So damned good!

American golf legend Arnold Palmer has died at the age of 87. I don't like golf one little bit, but as he was among the sport's all time greats I thought his passing deserved a mention here.

I've been playing more superb CDs – Live Rust (Neil Young and Crazy Horse in concert), Bad Company's first album and a treasured early 1970's Fleetwood Mac Greatest Hits set featuring classic cuts from the Peter Green era when they were British blues rock heroes.

September 28 – England football manager Sam Allardyce has quit the job he claims he'd always dreamed of having – after just 67 days and one match in charge.

Why? – because, metaphorically speaking, he's been caught with his trousers down.

Big Sam, 61, apparently told undercover newspaper reporters how to "get around" rules on player transfers. He's also said to have used his role to strike a deal worth £400,000 to represent a Far East firm.

A Football Association statement called Allardyce's conduct "inappropriate" and the man himself has accepted he made a "significant error of judgement", for which he's apologized.

He blamed "entrapment" for the fact he'd been exposed acting "silly."

Gareth Southgate, the under-21s manager, will oversee the senior side's next four matches – World Cup qualifiers against Malta and Slovenia in October, Scotland in November and a friendly against Spain also that month. The next game after that is in March.

September 29 – Wishing a very happy birthday to my friend and former work colleague Lorna Lane – a beautiful person and first-class drinking buddy.

Israel's former prime minister and president Shimon Peres has died after suffering a massive stroke. He was 93.

Peres shared a Nobel Prize for jointly forging a peace deal between Israelis and Palestinians – yet the fighting between them flared up again and continues. Perhaps they could now lay down their arms for good in his memory? Just a thought.

September 30 – I've managed to get hold of a second-hand copy of an excellent compilation CD by Zodiac Mindwarp and the Love Reaction that kicks off with the mighty Prime Mover and continues with some very potent hard and heavy rock and roll.

I've also finally secured a CD of On Stage, the brilliant live album by Rainbow from the days when Ronnie James Dio was on vocals. I had it on cassette once and it was terrific driving music – one of the finest live albums ever made. I've been after it on CD for several years.

I'm playing it now and it's so wonderfully kick ass it's simply impossible not to get up from typing at times to move around and rock out to it. Heavy blues rock at its very best.

For my money, it stands alongside Thin Lizzy's Live and Dangerous, Simple Minds in the City of Light, Frampton Comes Alive, Deep Purple's Made in Japan and Led Zep's the Song Remains the Same as a shining example of a great act in concert. Yeah, that damned good!

Neil Young's Live Rust, All the World's a Stage by Rush, Iron Maiden's Death on the Road, Bob Marley Live at the Lyceum and the Band's Last Waltz also warrant a mention here.

As do Pink Floyd's Pulse, If You Want Blood You've Got It by AC/DC, Yessongs by Yes, Live at Wembley by Queen, Haarp by Muse, Live at Last (Black Sabbath), One Night at Budokan (the Michael Schenker Group) and Motorhead's No Sleep Till Hammersmith.

And Tom Petty's Pack up the Plantation, Seconds Out (Genesis), Welcome Back My Friends (Emerson, Lake and Palmer), the Beatles at the Hollywood Bowl and the Doors in Concert.

Then of course, there's the Rolling Stones' Get Yer Ya-Ya's Out, Peter Tosh Captured Live, Bruce Springsteen 1975–1985, Wings Over America and the sublime Who Live at Leeds.

While acquiring the Mindwarp and Rainbow CDs, I also picked up Billy Fury's Hit Parade, a Foreigner compilation and Reet Petite, Jackie Wilson's prime cuts. Quality music or what?

It's Friday now and I've thoroughly enjoyed all five of these albums since buying them in Boscombe on Wednesday. I've also been playing Hawkwind's magnificent In Search of Space again – a CD I already had in my collection. I revel in delicious sounds.

October 2 – More than 70 people have been injured, four seriously, in a gas blast in Spain. It happened in a cafe near Malaga city about 5pm local time yesterday, during a festival.

October 3 – Well, it's Monday morning and I've spent another highly satisfactory weekend with friends.

Friday it was off to Sam and Carl's for drinkies with them, Jem Hannen and Tina Mcauley.

Saturday evening I went to my friend Jaymi Darragh's 40th birthday bash at the Iford Bridge Tavern, on the border of Bournemouth and Christchurch – walking distance from here.

I've known Jaymi for years. She lives just round the corner from me and has been a very good mate, supportive in both emotional and practical ways.

It was great to see her again and also our mutual pal Emily Perry, who once worked behind the bar at the Bell. Emily's a thinker, like me, and we used to have long, detailed discussions in between her stints cleaning, tidying and shelf stocking during the quiet daytime sessions.

Both women seemed delighted to see me and gave me heart-warming hugs.

So did current Bell bar manager Nicola Williams when I saw her off-duty in the pub. It's so nice to be embraced by lovely ladies!

My Bell visit last night ended the weekend well in the company of many mates including Matt Brant, John Gaynor, John Palmer, Mark Hemington, Penny Williams (another hug), Shannon Hanlon, Simon Turnbull, Ruth Troke, Victoria Brown, Mark Thornton, Sean Phillips, Mikey and Lou Delahaye, Brian, Darren, bar staff Lottie Wragg and Tony Jeffery and DJ Ross Maslin. Excellent!

October 4 – Blimey! Another explosion – this time in Syria, fatal and apparently deliberate.

At least 22 people were killed and dozens hurt in a blast at a Kurdish wedding in Hasaka yesterday (Tuesday). So far it's unclear whether it was caused by a remote controlled device or a suicide bomber.

But a statement by the ISIL-affiliated Amaq news agency said a man had attacked a gathering of Kurdish fighters on the edge of the city using machine guns and an explosive vest.

Hasaka is mainly in the hands of the YPG – the Kurdish protection force – after it evicted the Syrian army in August.

ISIL – the Islamic State of Iraq and the Levant – also claimed responsibility for suicide attacks in the Syrian city of Hama on Monday that killed three people and wounded 11.

Two men wearing explosive-laded belts struck near the ruling Baath party office and a police station, Amaq reported.

Meanwhile, it appears peace talks have broken down between the USA and Russia over Syria's civil war. Bad news!

October 4, 4.30pm – Just had a great afternoon in the Bell with my "adopted daughter" Nicola Williams, Shannon "Smiler" Hanlon, Kelly Adams, Dave Froud, Darren and Steve.

You hate this frigging system but stuff it, harsh needs must
You can't stand all the falsehood but you have to grab a crust.

October 5 – Happy birthday to my ex-wife Joe, her twin sister Cheryl and my daughter-in-law Emily. Hope you all have a wonderful day.

At least six people have died – and more fatalities are expected to be revealed – as the wildest hurricane in a decade has ripped through the Caribbean.

Four are known to have been killed in the Dominican Republic and two in Haiti. This sad toll is expected to rise as authorities assess the extent of Hurricane Matthew's devastation.

The Category Four storm has now moved off the north-eastern coast of Cuba, heading towards Florida. But early reports suggest Cuba hasn't been as badly affected as Haiti.

Matthew is the latest natural disaster to hit our planet. But there are plenty of man-made tragedies for folk to contend with too.

For example, more than 100 children are among 338 people losing their lives in heavy bombardment of the Syrian city of Aleppo in recent times. The strikes were a joint effort by the country's government and Russia. Aleppo, held by rebels, has also been attacked by home-grown groups allied with the Syrian authorities.

It's a bitter, bloody civil war that seems to have no end.

Then there's the Congo, where nearly five million have died in the past four and a half years due to that land's own internal fighting – a tragic crisis barely mentioned in western media.

"This is the worst calamity in Africa this century and one which the world has consistently found reasons to overlook" said the International Rescue Committee's David Johnson yesterday.

In our national news, UK Independence Party's new leader Diane James has quit after just 18 days in the job, saying she hasn't felt she's had the full support of members.

What a total farce this ridiculous political party is proving to be as it implodes amid internal bickering. Fit for government? – That's a laugh! Its disarray is good news for our country.

October 6 – Unhinged, immigrant-baiting buffoon Nigel Farage is temporarily back in charge of UKIP. Now there's a surprise!

Hurricane Matthew is now heading for the United States, where nervous residents are battening down the hatches. It's known to have killed more than 22 people so far.

And Theresa May has given her first keynote speech as Prime Minister to the Conservative Party conference in Birmingham.

In a televised address patently aimed at moderate Labour voters as much as Tory ones, she laid out her vision for a United Kingdom run for the benefit of all, not just a privileged few.

Gone was the hard-line right-wing rhetoric of Cameron, Osborne and Thatcher. Instead, we saw a soft, conciliatory middle-ground approach lacking the hateful, cruel, unfair, unjust and divisive attitudes of previous Conservative leaders that have led to so much pain and misery.

This is to be welcomed, of course. But as always the proof of the pudding is in the eating. I guess we'll just have to wait and see if May's actions reflect her refreshingly restrained, positive and encouraging words.

Especially in light of her own past record, including a recent stint as Home Secretary, when she seemed to be just as obnoxiously right-wing, aloof and uncaring as cabinet colleagues.

But so far, so good. I don't want the Conservatives in power but if they are I'd much rather have her in the driving seat than the god-awful Thatcher or Cameron – if her declarations are to be believed that is. And that is the million dollar question.

You may have noticed that in recent months I haven't been banging on quite so much about politics or blasting the shocking comments and behaviour of our cold and cruel leaders.

This is precisely because of May's less aggressive, lower-profile stance – a lot more reasoned and far less arrogant, spiteful and in your face than the high-handed and callous Cameron.

Consequently, I've been nowhere near as infuriated or motivated to comment or retaliate.

October 7 – And yet more birthdays! My pal Sam Excell's son Rudy is six today. His brother Alex is 22 tomorrow and it was their auntie Diane's 60th on Wednesday, so I'm off to Sam's later for a triple birthday party involving family, friends, cards presents, cakes and a buffet.

Three million US citizens have been warned to evacuate their homes as Hurricane Matthew is poised to hit Florida hard. It's already killed about 300 across the Caribbean and Cuba.

The crazy gang – official name UKIP – stays in the news thanks to an alleged punch-up among its MEPs that ended with one of them hospitalized. They're trying to play it down, but this seems to suggest that they have thugs as well as raving bigots in their midst. Nice!

As for Labour, Jeremy Corbyn has reshuffled his front bench team, with the likeable Diane Abbott taking over as shadow home secretary following Andy Burnham's resignation to concentrate on being the party's candidate in the Greater Manchester mayoral election.

I've been playing a range of music over the past couple of day – as per usual – including Deep Purple, the Verve and Bad Company (second album, Straight Shooter, this time).

October 8 – Happy birthday Alex, good to see you at yesterday's bash mate. It was a fine affair as it goes, with him, his dad Russell, mum Sam, Carl, Rudy, Bailey, Bec (very briefly), Tina Mcauley, Diane, her daughter Kirsty, Kelly Adams and her children and Jem Hannen.

And of course the two mad mutts Albert and Bramble, adding to the glorious chaos.

The death toll from Hurricane Matthew has now reached 900. Blimey!

October 9 – Happy birthday John Lennon. The peace campaigner and former Beatle would have been 76 has he lived and not been shot dead outside his New York apartment in 1980.

Yesterday was one of contrasting fortunes and mixed emotions for yours truly. A friend I was due to have an evening meal with at a nearby Indian restaurant contacted me in the morning to report that her mum has just died unexpectedly.

Stunned and disappointed, I expressed my deep sympathy to my poor pal, lit a candle for her mum and cancelled the table booking. This put the day on a right downer just as it had begun.

We had planned to go to the Bell after the meal. Now at a loose end, I decided to go there anyway – and I'm so pleased I did because it lifted my mood quite spectacularly.

Celebration was in the air for birthday girls Hannah Nicol, an off-duty barmaid, and Sam Lowney, former Bell bar manager now working at a Southbourne pub-cum-restaurant.

It's actually Sam's birthday later in the month but she and hubby Dave will be away then on safari in Africa so they decided to hold her pub bash last night, three days before they jet off.

Jem Hannen, Penny and Nicola Williams, Mark Chastney, John Gaynor, Mark Evans, Laura Williams, Matt Brant, Mikey Delahaye, Krissie Benbow and Paul Clyde attended.

Also Tony Jeffery, Lottie Wragg, Tim Robbins, Stu and Melody Moss, Brian and Aussie Stu.

It was another fab evening in my beloved local with a whole load of beautiful people. Cool!

Oh, and excellent live music was supplied by the talented father and son duo Matt Black (piano, vocals) and Chris Payn (electric guitar).

Trees and power lines have been brought down, there's severe flooding and a million residents are without power as Hurricane Matthew pounds Florida, USA. And Haiti has declared three days of national mourning for its 900-plus citizens killed by the storm.

Closer to home, events are being held to mark the 50th anniversary of the disaster in Aberfan village, Wales, when a colliery tip collapsed, sliding into a school and homes to kill 116 children and 28 adults. It happened on October 21, 1966. Fifty years – doesn't seem it!

October 10 – And yet another birthday! This time Bell barmaid Lottie Wragg's 19th.

Lottie's good mate Demi Pitkin was working the bar alongside Tony Jeffery last night as I finished off the weekend in fine style with another pub visit.

Mark, Laura, Brian, Matt Brant and John Gaynor were there again, this time with Simon Turnbull, Ruth Troke, John Palmer, Kelly Adams, Billy Clarkson, Jenny Daniels, Ben Avill, Alex King, Shannon Hanlon, DJ Ross Maslin, Darren and the usual Sunday karaoke singers.

Seeing all those lovely ladies over the weekend meant I had more nice hugs. Sweet!

But I was well aware that another female friend was notably absent – the one who had been forced to pull out of that planned Indian meal rendezvous due to her mum's shocking sudden death. I really feel for her, poor woman.

The Welsh football team suffered a blow yesterday as they attempt to qualify for the 2018 World Cup – an embarrassing 1-1 draw against lowly Georgia. The Republic of Ireland fared better, beating Moldova 3-1.

The previous day, England's first match with Gareth Southgate in charge ended with a highly satisfactory 2-0 victory over Malta. Scotland, in the same group, drew 1-1 with Lithuania, so as things stand England are top of the group with two wins after two matches.

Northern Ireland, in world champions Germany's group, beat San Marino 4-0.

Calais resembles a fierce jungle due to the migrant crisis while tension grows between Russia and the USA as troops and weapons are mobilized escalating World War Three. Ye gods!

****

CHAPTER TEN

The Lesser Of Two Evils

October 12 – England's national football team stays top of its qualifying group after three matches in the lead-up to the 2018 World Cup – despite a dull, uninspiring goalless draw against Slovenia last night.

Southgate's strikers lacked fire power and our lads would have actually lost the game but for a brilliant performance by goalkeeper Joe Hart, who pulled off a series of terrific saves.

England retains pole position with seven points thanks to Scotland's 3-0 defeat by Slovakia. The Scots, with four points, slip to fourth behind Lithuania and Slovenia, each with five.

Northern Ireland went down 2-0 to current world champions Germany, staying third in their group behind the German table toppers and second-placed Azerbaijan. The Irish Republic sits second in its group with Wales in third place.

I had another good Tuesday afternoon in the pub yesterday with Nicola, Mikey, Mark, Laura, puppy dog Flick and Darren. And on the way home I saw Nicola's mum Penny, walking up the road having just finished work at the Nationwide Southbourne branch, where I bank.

It's just occurred to me that some folk perusing my odd ramblings won't know the family and friends I name check with considerable frequency, and might well be wondering why I do it.

Well, it's because these individuals are a huge part of my unfolding life story. They've made the whole experience bearable – and at times a lot of fun – so it's my way of saying thanks.

Not to refer to them would be very strange indeed – especially when there's a good chance they might well at some point read at least part of one or more of my dozen published books.

I also make regular, detailed mentions of my favourite writers and music and comedy stars plus their brilliant work. These folk have similarly enhanced my existence with their talent.

And, to put it bluntly, this is my journey and my journal so if anyone don't like it – tough!

I've been revisiting the rather splendid Beatles album Let It Be – the 2003 Naked version, of course. Like many fans, I much prefer this purer, more basic and honest interpretation of the long player than the over-produced 1970 Phil Spector original with its orchestra and choir.

There are some cracking good songs here, including Don't Let Me Down, oddly and disappointingly omitted by Spector for some reason.

At the moment I'm savouring the succulent delights of the Genesis Platinum Collection triple CD set. Excellent!

And now, a short summary of the daytime Jeremy Kyle TV programme – "On today's show, a bunch of idiots who deserve each other and everything they get, and shouldn't receive help of any kind." Says it all, really. But it's still inexplicably compulsive viewing – funny, that.

Okay, fair enough, before anyone says it, I fully accept that some of Kyle's guests should get a break and a helping hand – including the hopeless drink, drug and gambling addicts and those with severe depression, serious anger issues, the abused, disabled or disadvantaged.

But I would ask if this sensationalist TV show, with its high ratio of obnoxious, unstable participants and outrageously biased and unbelievably egocentric host, is the best way to tackle such sensitive and sometimes taboo issues? I'd argue not – no freaking way!

I applaud Graham Stanier and his aftercare team who do such sterling work in identifying, addressing and dealing with people's problems. But stuff Kyle, he's just a self-obsessed knob who loves the drama – exploiting others' pain and misery to boost his own profile.

For some, including me, this mad drive for notoriety backfires hugely as he ends up looking unhinged, big headed, petty, spiteful and more than a little ridiculous. But many love him.

Most of his guests really are morons. The same applies to his compliant, undiscerning studio audience for that matter. Makes me despair, really – where the Hell do they get these people?

Speaking of horrible individuals, the run-up to the USA presidential election is getting very nasty and ugly with Democrat candidate Hillary Clinton and Republican rival Donald Trump exchanging insults during televised debates.

Billionaire businessman Trump is being portrayed as a devious fraudster and a sexist pig, and Clinton as a woman guilty of very serious misconduct and deeply shady activities.

It seems American citizens must choose the lesser of two dreadful evils – and either of them could accelerate our slide into World War Three to a headlong pelt. Gordon frigging Bennett!

October 13 – The Congo, Syria, Gaza, the Ukraine, Afghanistan, Calais... Russia and the USA squaring up for a major clash... terrorism... growing ethnic tension at home and abroad... widespread ruthless and violent abuse... homelessness... wars, famine, death and misery...

...and what does our media prattle on about? People dressing up as clowns in a new craze and a price war over Marmite! Bloody Hell – talk about insanely messed up priorities!

Don't get me wrong – I'm all for a bit of light relief to offset all the nasty negative stuff. I'm very keen to see more heart-warming stories of human courage, compassion, resilience and achievement to offset the ugly, upsetting tales of the far too widespread violence and cruelty.

But we're not getting this with our pathetic telly and newspaper coverage here or across the globe. Real news of shocking events and circumstances in the Congo, Gaza or Afghanistan is often ignored as we're fed insubstantial drivel and endless sex scandals. It's a disgrace!

Yes, we certainly should be told of disasters, crises and people's atrocious treatment of others on small or large scales – but this has to be balanced by frequent mentions of the far more positive aspects of human interaction that often go unreported and are therefore overlooked.

We definitely shouldn't have our headlines dominated by garbage about clown costumes and Marmite, or tedious blanket coverage of sexual behaviour – socially accepted or otherwise – in an obsessive and titillating way that degrades genuine issues and insults our sensibilities.

I've said it before and I'll continue to do so until it ceases to be true – it's hardly surprising that so many folk have seriously warped ideas of reality and normality when they're constantly bombarded with such ludicrous versions of both.

Appropriately enough, an item of today's TV news centred on the latest breakthrough in gaming technology that allows enthusiasts to more effectively operate in a virtual reality setting through the use of a cutting-edge high-tech headset.

Flippin' 'eck! – Talk about further bending rules and perceptions to leave people completely confused over the nature of reality – already an incredibly subjective matter I've found.

And they called John Lennon nuts for saying he considered his dreams to be as real as his wide awake experiences. I can see exactly what he meant. And if you can't, I despair!

I watched another fascinating documentary on You Tube last night that debunked the daft old claim that Sir Paul McCartney actually died in a 1966 car crash to be replaced by a look-alike. This is palpable nonsense, proving what total cobblers can pass for fact nowadays.

Also on telly last night, I viewed three disturbing BBC Three programmes on the network's catch-up service. (The channel is no longer on normal TV since going primarily online.)

All three documentaries highlighted hatred. One was about a fire and brimstone American pastor who equated homosexuality with paedophilia and said all "sexual perverts" should die.

The second featured a xenophobic group of gun-toting right-wing extremists who took a similar attitude to blacks in general and Muslims in particular. The third asked the pertinent question – is Britain racist? – coming to the shocking conclusion it still was.

I was left reeling, wondering if I was still actually living in the 21st century or had somehow inexplicably slipped back into the 1950s.

I thought we'd got past all that bigoted nonsense years ago. Apparently not – in fact it seems to be returning with a vengeance. And I find that worrying and depressing in the extreme.

Today I've been listening to CDs by three very good local bands – the Bonsai Pirates, Mischa and his Merry Men and now Galahad. We really do have a wealth of talent in this area!

October 15 – Had a fab time at Sam and Carl's yesterday with them, the boys, the dogs, Becca, Tina Mcauley, Diane, her daughter Kirsty, Kirsty's bloke Billy, Kelly Adams and her daughter Storm. Super duper!

TV legend Jean Alexander has died aged 90. She starred in two of the world's all-time great small screen shows; BBC's Last of the Summer Wine and ITV's Coronation Street, in which she played the waspish curler-wearing Hilda Ogden brilliantly for more than two decades.

October 16 – Good news for AFC Bournemouth fans – the Cherries walloped Hull 6-1 yesterday to shoot up to 9th in the

Premier League. And a big bonus for me personally is that Slough Town stay top of the Evo-stik southern premier league by a five-point margin.

It was great to see my friend Martine Phillips Hannen – Jem's daughter – at the Bell last night. Jem was also there, along with John Palmer, Sarah and Darren Spence, Krissie Benbow, Paul Clyde, Mark Evans, Laura Williams, John Gaynor, Tim Robbins, Lottie Wragg, Mikey Delahaye, Ollie Okoye, Stu and Melody Moss and our mates Jim and Brian.

October 17 – Laura, Mark, Jem, John G, Mikey and Krissie were also in the bar last night, on this occasion accompanied by Nicola Williams, Mark Chastney, Matt Brant, Gemma Jones, Tony Jeffery, Shannon Hanlon, Demi Pitkin, Billy Clarkson and Kelly Adams. Cool!

October 18 – Happy birthday to my friend Lisa Byrom-Papas, one of the Bell's "old crowd" who no longer drinks there regularly so I hardly see her these days.

October 18, 5pm –Speaking of the Bell, I've just had my usual Tuesday sesh there with some beautifully talented people – Laura Williams (writer), Krissie Benbow (artist), Nicola Williams, Mark Evans, Ben Avill, Alex King, Shannon Hanlon, Harry Evans and others.

I love making new friends but I also love re-connecting with people I've not seen or spoken to for years or even decades. Having friends and family is what makes life worth living.

Some mates very close to us emotionally have chosen to move away, hundreds of miles in certain cases, so are no longer part of our everyday lives. But they stay in our hearts.

Others take their places in the physical sense, but you still love them all just the same – or at least I do. Consequently it's very upsetting – heartbreaking even – when you lose contact or, worse still, inadvertently anger or sadden a pal by misreading their circumstances and needs.

You know it wouldn't have happened if they still lived close by and you could support them in person. But the distance between you and years apart take huge tolls not always obvious.

In many ways the experiences you've had in the interim have inevitably changed you both so you're no longer the same people you were.

And you haven't seen those changes take place first hand as events have unfolded. You haven't been able to feel each other's pain – or happiness – quite so acutely.

Result? Severe misunderstandings can badly undermine your friendship so that by the time you realize how badly you've handled a delicate, emotionally-charged situation from afar, it's too bloody late. Remoteness can be a real curse.

Apologizing doesn't work because the damage is done and can't be repaired. That's life, I guess, but it's sad and frustrating all the same. It happened to me recently and hurts a lot.

October 19 – And another birthday! This really is a busy month for them. This time it's Sam Rose Lowney, currently on safari in Africa enjoying a belated honeymoon with hubby Dave.

I've been watching a new Adam Curtis film on BBC iPlayer. Called *HyperNormalisation*, it's as brilliant, enlightening and thought-provoking as his others. I thoroughly endorse it.

And I'd especially recommend it to anyone puzzled and staggered by the mess our world's in – the Middle East, the Ukraine, a looming global economic crash, slide into World War Three and so on – because it lays out 50 years of history leading up to our current fraught situation.

As usual, Curtis ties together many apparently unconnected issues, including the recent EU referendum, financial instability, dirty politics, hippy ideals and LSD use and virtual reality into a coherent, absorbing summary of why we're faced with the huge problems we have.

It's all here – from Lockerbie to the Lebanon, Prozac to Palestine, tyrants to terrorism – in a mesmerizing three hour documentary made this year showing Curtis at his controversial best.

He tells how computer technology and the internet have been employed to help twist people's concepts of reality in what he calls "managed perception."

He maintains that the current Syrian civil war and the so-called Arab Spring are the inevitable outcomes of the ruthless, opportunistic exploitation of situations, events and nations' leaders.

The cast of characters includes Libya's Colonel Gaddafi, Iran's Ayatollah Khomeini, Iraq's Saddam Hussein and Syria's father and son presidents Hafez and Bashar al-Assad.

Vladimir Putin, Donald Trump, Henry Kissinger, Tony Blair, Ronald Reagan, Islamic State, and the internet-driven 2011 occupation of Wall Street by angry protesters also feature.

And Curtis fascinatingly suggests that the whole UFO issue over the past half century or so has been a huge hoax masking the use of top secret, high-tech military aircraft, nothing to do with extra-terrestrials' spaceships.

Along with cyber space chicanery and drug use – prescribed or not – he points to disaster movies about alien invasions and major catastrophes as other examples of the deliberate blurring of the lines between fact and fiction intended to confuse, scare and manipulate us all.

Needless to say politicians, business and banking bosses and other society big shots end up looking pretty bad – as usual in Adam Curtis productions. He hasn't lost his touch – good!

Thank the stars that, swamped as we are with biased media reports, blatant propaganda and the deliberately distorted version of reality he highlights, we desperately need intelligent and probing, refreshingly discerning truth seeking journalists like him. Power to his elbow I say.

Battle Scars by Galahad and Tom Petty's Greatest Hits have been on my CD player as I've typed today's journal entry. Absolutely spiffing!

October 20 – British forces have been bombing targets in Mosul, Iraq, in a bid to drive Islamic State out of the city and help the Iraqi Army restore control to a native population welcoming the move with open arms. Well, that's what we're being told anyway.

But, as always, many of us wonder if this is the real truth or just the cover story in this Lewis Carroll world where reality is twisted and nothing is quite as it appears.

This latest so-called news report from the war-torn Middle East ties in so nicely with what I was going to write here anyway – before seeing it on BBC television this morning.

Which is – thinking a bit more about that Adam Curtis film, I've been recalling an earlier one of his called Bitter Lake, with its themes overlapping those of the new production.

In both, Curtis traces the roots of current crises, including the rise in violent Islamic fundamentalism, back decades to just after the Second World War.

That, of course, was when the Zionist State of Israel was aggressively set up in a predominantly Muslim area of the globe – a provocative act if ever there was one.

But it's also when the USA struck a deal with Saudi Arabia that's had huge repercussions ever since. Basically, it was "You let us buy your oil and we'll leave your religion alone."

That religion was a savage, intolerant, backward-looking form of Islam called Wahhabism which largely rejected the Western way of doing things, seeing it as inefficient and corrupt.

Wahhabism spread – taking root and flourishing in various neighbouring countries including Pakistan and Afghanistan. As it grew, it spawned offshoots that became adopted by jihadists ("holy warriors") including modern-day ISIS fighters.

While all this was going on, Syrian president Hafez al-Assad (now deceased) introduced the concept of suicide bombers in his bid to unite the Arab nations and drive the Western powers, and especially the USA, out of the Middle East. His son Bashar now carries that torch.

And where's the Middle East close to? – Russia, once part of the now-collapsed USSR which bordered the volatile area where so-called Islamic, Judaic and Christian nut jobs often fight.

The Soviet empire (USSR) and now Russia, have both consistently been eager to side with Arab leaders battling Western ideologies seen as seriously flawed – evil even.

Brutal dictators have been tolerated – and in some cases actively supported – by both sides as the old capitalist versus communist Cold War raged, threatening a global catastrophe.

Russia is still as heavily involved in places like Libya and Syria as either the USA or Britain – but often on the opposite side of violent clashes. Just as in Korea and Vietnam in the past.

Islam itself is historically split into two frequently warring factions – Sunni and Shia – leading to bloody conflicts over the centuries that continue to this day.

Throw Colonel Gaddafi, Saddam Hussein, the Ayatollah Khomeini and Osama bin Laden into the mix, facing up to Reagan, Blair, the Bushes and others promoting Western ideas and ambitions, and you have an unstable melting pot and a recipe for disaster time and time again.

And we must constantly bear in mind that we're seeing all this through the fractured, buckled lens of a false conventional reality, presented to us as truth by those in charge of everything.

****

CHAPTER ELEVEN
Modern Systems

October 21 – Technology can be a right pain in the arse sometimes.

I find it so ruddy ironic that devices designed to aid communication can sometimes damage it so badly.

Missed calls, unanswered texts and misunderstood messages can cause frustration and friction to the point of wrecking relationships.

I have a natural aversion to lengthy text or phone conversations or long-winded back-and-forth messaging of any kind. I much prefer face to face contact – the human touch.

I keep my mobile switched off most of the time, checking it once, maybe twice a day. I access Facebook through my bulky computer system that dominates one corner of my living room – again, once or twice daily.

That way, I can actually live a life and get other things done without constantly feeling the need to answer calls or messages, getting drawn into distracting, time-eating activities that I find far too cold and clinical. That would do my head in. I crave close-up personal warmth.

I have no desire to accept others' offers of joining messenger or Skype systems – the first would be pointless and the second a truly dreadful, highly irritating mockery of proper face-to-face dialogue.

Some may conclude, wrongly, that I'm being evasive or unsociable. Not so – I just want my relationships to be conducted in the flesh. Maybe the fact I live alone has relevance here.

The days of letter writing to those living miles away are well and truly over, which I feel is very sad. Am I showing my age? Well, maybe, but I believe in the old-fashioned concept of human interaction unhindered by mass-produced gizmos.

Sure, Facebook is an excellent way of maintaining links with family and friends when I'm not with them in the physical sense. But it's no substitute for the real thing.

I have a particular reason to be resentful of modern technology right now, as I swear it massively contributed to the unfortunate misunderstanding that recently ruined a long-standing very close friendship with someone who now lives hundreds of miles away.

As a Green party member, I'm all for protecting the environment, but I can't help thinking that if we'd kept in contact via pen-on-paper letters – as we once did – our friendship would probably have survived unharmed.

The fact it's been torn to ribbons is tragic. I messed up for sure but I refuse to take all the responsibility. Bleeding technology is as much to blame. Facebook brought us back together but in the end modern systems helped tear us apart. I've learned a tough lesson.

It's the Aberfan anniversary today so I've lit a candle for the victims and their families.

Russian warships are sailing through the English Channel, apparently on their way to Syria. They're within international waters but this is being viewed as a very provocative act as tensions grow between their home country and the West. Our navy is keeping a close watch.

European leaders have strongly condemned Russia's involvement in the bombing of Aleppo.

He's a kamikaze Nazi full of hate and death
With explosives in his pocket and hot toxic breath.

On a brighter note, I'm off to Boscombe's O2 Academy tonight to see UB40 in concert.

October 22 – UB40 were great, and so was the company. I had a highly enjoyable evening with Carl Young, Jem Hannen, Mark Hemington, Penny Williams and Amy Wrixon.

It's the second time I've seen the band – the first being more than three decades ago at Poole on the Present Arms tour, mentioned before and still one of the best gigs I've ever attended.

Some members have left and been replaced over the years but the group is still driven by the mighty rhythm section of founder members Jimmy Brown (drums) and Earl Falconer (bass).

Robin Campbell (vocals, guitar), Brian Travers (saxophone) and Norman Hassan (trombone, vocals) have also been stalwarts since UB40 formed in Birmingham in 1978, and remain so.

It was a superb gig as the legendary reggae outfit tried to please all their fans – those, like me, who prefer the harder-edged, self-penned, politically-charged songs from the first two albums to lovers of the later, poppier covers that cemented their global success.

Red Red Wine, Kingston Town and I Can't Help Falling in Love with You predictably got the crowd singing along – but so did the brilliant Tyler and King, both from the early days.

Signing Off was a terrific debut long-player but the follow-up, Present Arms, remains my favourite of theirs – reggae at its very best. And Present Arms in Dub, the heavier version of it I also possessed at one time, is mind-blowingly exquisite.

Personally, I would have preferred more of the social conscience and deep dub they excelled at than the softer pop they're most famous for – but it was still a superb show all the same.

Oh, and I bought a tour tee-shirt.

October 22, six hours later – Just had a fab time thanks to a visit from the family, namely Chloe, Harvey, Emily, Phil and Oscar the teddy bear (a temporarily adopted member from Chloe's preschool). Sweet!

October 23 – Sat in the Commodore Hotel having a meal with the family yesterday, chomping through bangers and mash and gazing out over a sparkling sun-kissed sea, I thought of those Russian warships in the Channel. I mentioned this to Phil and Emily.

A train of thought led me to later muse on other provocative gestures, such as militant Islamists saying they won't rest until their flag flies over 10 Downing Street and our country is run according to Sharia law – a strict interpretation of their religious codes of practice.

Many people are infuriated by this statement, seeing it as highly inflammatory. The general view seems to be "This is a Christian nation guided by the Bible and the Ten Commandments and if you don't like it you can sod off elsewhere because we will never bow to your wishes."

This is a totally understandable knee-jerk reaction to a proposal that would fly in the face of centuries of tradition. And as a creature of routine who doesn't like change, I tend to concur.

Our way of life is far from perfect but it's ours dammit – and its history and familiarity make it kinda reassuring. Better the devil you know and all that.

But hold it right there – when we analyse this argument more diligently, without preconceptions or bias, we must ask ourselves if it really stands up to close scrutiny.

You could say we actually ceased being a Christian country ages ago. We're multi-cultural – always have been – and even those who still pay lip service to that religion and its rules governing behaviour often fail to back words with actions – regularly doing the opposite.

As for the Ten Commandments, they seem to be broken with alarming frequency. And they're not exclusively Christian anyway – Jews and Muslims also revere Bible teachings and, apart from the first two, they echo the edicts of the far older Egyptian Book of the Dead.

For those who don't know, Commandment One is "I am the Lord thy God" and Two is "Thou shalt have no other gods" – both reflecting the monotheistic nature of the world's three big faiths – as opposed to the pantheon of Egyptian, Roman, Greek and other pagan deities.

All this begs the question – would a country run according to Muslim principles really be any worse than what we're currently lumbered with? It all depends on how strictly that law is enforced of course – and Sharia does seem extreme. The same applies to any set of rules.

So when all's said and done, I do share others' grave concern that what's being referred to by the Sharia law exponents is an intolerant, brutal interpretation of Islamic codes of conduct.

Turning from religion to friendship, but staying with ethical behaviour, I'd like to now air a few thoughts on the nature of mate etiquette.

It can be nice, flattering even, when people regard you highly enough to trust you with sensitive information. But it can backfire on you in a horrid way.

Pals of mine recently confided in me about something that we all knew would cause huge ructions and deep hurt when later revealed.

I respected my mates' wish for secrecy, as I always would in such circumstances. I like to be viewed as reliable and discreet, a good egg.

But when the cat sprang from the bag in spectacular fashion, another friend who was emotionally devastated by the fallout turned on me, blasting me and asking bitterly if I was proud to have been part of the subterfuge.

Friggin' Hell, I thought, I didn't ask to be put in that terrible position in the first place!

I actually, genuinely felt for that poor, distraught injured party. But to have alerted them would have betrayed my other chums. I was in a no-win situation.

Some might jump in here declaring it's a question of loyalty – I should have chosen which side to be on. This is outrageously simplistic and besides, I don't work that way. I try not to hurt or anger anyone who's done me no harm.

I'd assert that actually, if my mates who confided in me had thought that much of me or stopped to consider my feelings, they wouldn't have compromised my integrity that way.

They should have dealt with the matter themselves and come clean to those adversely affected by their actions without involving me at all.

We all need to share our deepest concerns with close companions at times. We all seek support and advice when troubled. I like being a loved, respected friend and confidante.

But on this occasion, it was wrong to drag me in without giving me a chance to air my deep worry and reservations. Having been told of the situation, I would have advised my pals to sort it out post haste with others in the scenario. Sadly, I never got that opportunity.

As this unfortunate turn of events proved, you can't please all the people all the time – even though I do try, constantly. At the end of the day you can just do your best.

Another hard truth of this whole, tricky friendship lark is that we can all screw up now and then with bad judgement calls, poor timing and failure to properly grasp people's needs.

That's life, I guess.

Speaking of friends, yesterday evening continued a pretty awesome weekend with my visit to the Bell where I saw and chatted to John Palmer, John Gaynor, Jem Hannen, Laura Williams, Mark Evans, Stu and Melody Moss, Ruth Troke, Simon Turnbull, Mark

Chastney, Kelly Adams, Billy Clarkson, Alex King and others. Loved it!

October 24 – T'was great to see my good buddy Darren Williams in the pub last night, along with Jem Hannen, John Gaynor, Sean Phillips, Tony Jeffery, Lottie Wragg, Gemma Jones, Ross Maslin, Mark Evans and Laura Williams. Rounded off a terrific weekend appropriately!

Darren's loaned me a CD he's recently acquired. I've just played it once and it's so good I'm going to play it again straightaway. Called Echoes of Our Times, it's by Shakin' Stevens.

I know, I know – before you say it, I thought that too. Shakin' Stevens? Are you sure? But I'm actually deadly serious. Issued this year, it's superb and I'd thoroughly recommend it.

Forget Green Door, You Drive Me Crazy, This Ol' House and that cheesy Christmas song and video wheeled out every December. This album is 68-year-old Shaky's masterpiece – the crowning moment of his long career, the best thing he's done by a merry mile.

I always preferred his early stuff with the Sunsets anyway, belting out rock'n'roll classics. But this mesmerising, eye-opening collection takes him into a new league entirely.

These are folksy, earthy, roots-influenced compositions about the Welshman's own family history, marrying excellent lyrics with great soft rock tunes tinged with bluegrass and gospel, performed with crispness and polish by a skilled and really tight band. Shaky plays banjo.

Album opener Down in the Hole takes us back to the tough times when his ancestors toiled away in Cornwall's grim copper and tin mines. The final track looks to a feared bleak future.

In between we get references to Shaky's great grandfather, a Methodist preacher, the singer's Salvation Army grandma's mission to help the disadvantaged, and his dad and uncles' front-line suffering in World War One, when his mum's brother was killed. He's buried at Ypres.

Family secrets and the suffering of children also feature on this outstanding CD, arguably a pretty damned cool concept album.

I borrowed and subsequently played it at Darren's suggestion because he was enthusiastically singing its praises and happened to have it in his car (he was being a good boy and only drank a couple of shandies, in case you were wondering).

When Jem joined us a bit later, he confirmed that Darren had played it to him without telling him who it was and he'd been similarly impressed. I thought that if these two fellers with impeccable musical tastes liked it, I would too. I wasn't disappointed. In fact I'm delighted.

Jimmy Perry, co-writer of the classic TV shows Dad's Army and Hi-de-Hi, has passed away aged 93 after a short illness. Regarded as a giant of British comedy, he will be sorely missed.

October 25 – Dozens of people are said to have died in an attack on a police training college in Quetta, Pakistan. Three people wearing suicide bomb vests are alleged to have entered the building and taken hostages. All three were killed, assert official sources.

Islamic State has apparently claimed responsibility but the authorities blame another militant group called Lashkar-e-Jhangvi.

Two men and two women have lost their lives on a ride at Dreamworld theme park, Queensland, Australia.

Clearance of the notorious "jungle" refugee camp at Calais continued yesterday as 2,300 migrants left on buses for reception areas elsewhere in France.

The Calais camp has become a symbol of Europe's migrant crisis with about 8,000 living in desperate and squalid conditions. Many want to reach the UK.

Controversial expansion of Heathrow Airport has seemingly been approved by a committee of government ministers – although Downing Street has yet to confirm this.

Closer to home, a female friend of mine is attending her mum's funeral today. I feel for her and I've lit a candle.

I'm off soon to meet my very good friend Paula for our four-weekly catch-up – this time at her local pub, the Cricketers' at Springbourne, a Bournemouth area north of Boscombe.

October 26 – My rendezvous with Paula for drinks, chat and laughs was as pleasant as ever.

Jubilations! – Two boxes have arrived of paperback versions of *Sunshine and Ice Volumes 10 (Glittering Stars), 11 (Amazing Messages)* and *12 (Humour and Miracles)*. I've started handing them out to mates and will today post copies to addresses afar.

You can get hold of my books through Amazon/Kindle, Waterstones, Abe Books and Bookfinder by tapping in "Sunshine and Ice by Martin Money." The Abe Books website tells me they're available in the UK, Ireland, Germany, Australia and the USA.

It also informs me that booksellers in those countries have rated my volumes, in 38 cases giving them a five-star maximum score, with four stars in a further 15 instances. How cool!

And according to Bookfinder, my work is also on sale in France, Italy and Canada. Terrific!

I'm calling this latest outing Volume Z, Layers of Perception. I'm not overly superstitious but, well, just to be on the safe side, eh?

The first few instalments of *Sunshine and Ice* were published by Indepenpress, who then went bust. Author Essentials took over briefly, but stopped trading when the CEO died.

My books are now in the hands of New Generation Publishing of Olney, Bucks – head office Fleet Street, London.

What have I been playing this week? UB40 of course – the excellent Present Arms album (several times) and The Best of, Volume One – better than Two with its later, poppier songs.

October 29, 1.30pm – Just had a traumatic time visiting my seriously ill buddy Steve Yarwood in hospital. He's had a blood disease and liver problems for a few years now but his health has deteriorated fast in recent months He's really close to the end.

Poor Steve, who is younger than me, was rushed into the Royal Bournemouth on Thursday – two days ago. He has an infection and other complications, is dosed full of morphine and hooked up to all sorts of machines, drowsy as Hell and unable to speak.

Making him comfortable is all the nurses can do at this stage. It's a matter of days now at most. Jem, bless him, gave me a lift to the hospital and back so we could both see our great mate and let him know we were there for him.

Steve is one of the closest male friends I've ever had. We've known each other over 20 years and have had some right good chuckles together, laced with sarcasm, irreverence and dark humour. We relished our boozy, crazy "Tuesday night club" sessions at my flat. Happy days!

Jem joined in these for a while and at one time we were the three musketeers, meeting up in each others' homes to drink, smoke and wisecrack and going out for alcohol-based day trips.

It's heartbreaking to see Steve looking so thin, drawn, grey and helpless and to realize with great shock and sadness that we're so near to saying our last goodbyes in this reality.

October 30 – Steve passed away this morning. What a good job Jem and I got the chance to see him one last time yesterday. I'm devastated. He was my buddy, my bro. I've lit a candle and will be putting a little tribute on Facebook.

I have many, many terrific memories of my experiences with that man. We had such a laugh together. Now it's time for tears – but I know what he'd say about that!

Farewell, treasured friend. You are irreplaceable. You may be gone from us on this level, but your spirit will forever reside in the hearts of your family and friends. RIP, you grumpy, lovable git. I'm jointly dedicating this book to you.

Went to Sam and Carl's yesterday evening for drinks and daftness – a great tonic in the circumstances. Jem Hannen, Tina Mcauley and Sam's relative Diane were also there.

October 31 – Happy Halloween folks, and happy birthday to my friend Jane Marshall.

Yesterday was a sad and traumatic one for me but Facebook during the day and the Bell last night both came up trumps, thank goodness, lifting my spirits no end.

Pals were amazingly supportive with lovely comments and numerous "likes" for my Facebook status about Steve. It was also great to be with mates in my local pub later.

It was the usual Sunday karaoke session and DJ Ross Maslin was good enough to grant my request of playing a record by the Bloodhound Gang in a break between singers and dedicating it to my buddy, who loved the group. I bought Ross a pint as a "thank-you."

Other mates were just as kind. John Gaynor, Victoria Brown, Mark Thornton, Matt Brant, Scott Collins, landlady Laura Williams, Alex King, Lottie Wragg, Gemma Jones and Darren the window cleaner were there, and Jem arrived later, to my great relief.

I really was hoping he would turn up so we could raise a glass to our third musketeer mate on the day of his demise. Jem and I had a huge man hug. It had to be done. It was appropriate.

November 1 – Yesterday was the pagan festival of Halloween, today is the Christians' All Saints' Day and this morning we had more on the news about the controversial idea of running our country according to Sharia (Islamic) Law.

The problem, as I see it, is that those who advocate this the loudest are talking about a pretty extreme interpretation of Muslim rules and guidelines. I share others' concern over this.

I posed the question a few pages back – whether applying a moderate, compassionate reading of sound Muslim principles would be any worse than our current pseudo Christian system.

Let's face it, for centuries atheists and followers of other faiths in the UK have been expected to respect and forced to abide by a whole culture supposedly based on Christ's teachings – whether they liked it or not.

Some have quite rightly resented this denial of freedom, typified by the school assembly and echoed in Parliament, local councils, law courts and many businesses.

I welcome the relaxing of this rather oppressive regime to open it up to an acceptance of alternative religions and customs reflecting the reality of our multi-cultural society.

The last thing I want now is a replacement system just as intolerant and draconian but based on another faith – which I fear would be the end result of the Sharia Law zealots' ambitions.

Incidentally, there was also an item on today's telly news about banning footballers from wearing poppies on their shirts while playing matches on or near November 11. The reason given is that some see this as a political gesture that might offend certain folk.

But I don't see it as a political gesture at all. Neither is it a religious put-down. The fallen service folk we honour weren't all Christians. Some would have been atheists, some Jewish, some Muslim, Hindu, Buddhist, pagan and so on.

And they would have voted Tory, Labour, Liberal or none of them. War and death are no respecters of political or religious distinctions. To see poppies as an affront is ludicrous.

So is the warped mindset of some wearers who view them as a defiant and divisive gesture. You know, the dodgier, more militant factions of the "wear your poppy with pride" brigade.

Like millions of others, I buy and wear one every year and I've once again just changed my Facebook profile picture from a Halloween theme to a photo of a poppy growing in a field.

I don't do either out of any misguided concept of pride. I do both with a heavy heart – mourning the dead, respecting their sacrifices and yearning for war to end, permanently.

Pride – one of the Christian seven deadly sins – doesn't come into it. Unless, of course, you realize it's a major factor causing wars alongside ego, arrogance, ruthless ambition and greed.

Some idiots with their brains in their trousers would do well to recognize this truth.

November 1, evening – Thanks once again, Bell buddies. Went there this afternoon for my usual Tuesday daytime session with Nicola Williams, Mark Evans, Laura Williams, Mikey Delahaye, Harry Evans and a nice old feller called Joe. Just the ticket!

November 2 – I love the beauty and power of rock music in its diverse forms. It's thrilling, exciting, scintillating, sexy, profound, passionate, spirit-lifting, witty, enlightening and inspirational. Motorhead, Yes, UB40, Ellie Goulding, Eminem, the Clash… all of it.

Happy birthday to my friends Jenny Daniels and Helen Adams, two women I've met while drinking in the pub over the years. Jenny is my mate Ben Avill's girlfriend.

We're approaching Bonfire Night (Saturday November 5), the day we burn effigies and let off fireworks on the anniversary of the failed 1605 Gunpowder Plot to blow up Parliament.

It's also nearing Armistice Day (11th) and Remembrance Sunday (13th). We, the people, will never forget – unlike the politicians who cause wars then seem to have shocking memory lapses over their devastating consequences, constantly and criminally taking us into others.

Just listening to the brilliant Canadian indie band Arcade Fire on CD.

November 3 – England and Scotland's national football teams are set to defy a FIFA ruling by wearing black armbands emblazoned with poppies when they play each other in a World Cup qualifier next Friday, Armistice Day, November 11. Good – common sense prevails.

In issuing the "no poppies" edict, FIFA, the sport's global governing body, had quoted its rule preventing the display of emblems showing political preferences during fixtures.

Prime Minister Theresa May called the ban "utterly outrageous." I just think it's ridiculous. Political my backside! – Poppies honour and respect the fallen of all sides in wars, regardless of political, religious or cultural considerations. Or at least they do in my book.

Only right wing nuts with twisted ideas of national identity use them as a political statement – just as they do with the England flag and dear old St George. I say it's high time decent, peace-loving patriots seized them all back from these dolts dragging them through the dirt.

November 4, 11pm – Just back from the pub, where I realized – again – that raw emotion can hijack your life when you least expect it. Joy, despair, smiles, tears. You never forget and the pain still burns but the older you get; the more you can handle it. That's the theory, anyway.

November 6 – Yesterday was Bonfire Night and I went to a firework party at Sam and Carl's with punch, marshmallows, jacket spuds, chilli, sausages and sparklers. Good fun it was too – although it was freezing cold in the garden so I sought refuge in the warmth of the kitchen.

The children enjoyed it – Rudy, Bailey and Kelly Adams' kids Hudson and Storm – and the adults did too – Kelly, Becca, Cameron, Tina, Diane, Jem, Russell and Alex. Sweet!

November 6, 11pm – Just spent another super Sunday evening at the Bell with Nicola Williams, Mikey Delahaye, Matt Brant, John Gaynor, Jem Hannen, Jemma Davies, Shannon Hanlon, Guus Bruin, DJ Ross Maslin playing cool old school tunes and others. Great therapy!

Oh, and some impressive karaoke singers to boot.

November 8. 4pm – And another spirit-lifting session at my local pub. Thank you so much Nicola, Mikey, Mark, Laura, Harry, Ben and Joe. Splendid!

CD-wise, I've been enjoying The Doors in Concert, Pulse (Pink Floyd live), International Velvet (Catatonia), Ora (Rita Ora), the New Classic (Iggy Azalea) and Welcome to the Cheap Seats (a film soundtrack EP by The Wonder Stuff).

Meanwhile, in the USA, people have gone to the polls today to elect their new president – Donald Trump or Hillary Clinton. Ye gods – what a choice! They're both unstable, dangerous people so I fear either way an escalation of global conflict will result and we're all doomed.

Veteran broadcaster Jimmy Young has died aged 95. Mostly known as a Radio Two deejay for almost 30 years, he also interviewed the rich and famous. He started his long career as a pop star and had two number ones in 1955 – Unchained Melody and The Man from Laramie.

November 9 – Well, it's Trump and Facebook is full of people asking what the Hell the Americans have done electing him, fearing he will cause mayhem and spark World War Three.

I fear for us all too, but would have been just as nervous with Clinton as president. Both alternatives were frightening prospects. We were in a no-win situation.

As for the war, it's already here – but will most likely intensify. And that would have happened whichever of these dreadful liabilities was in the White House.

November 10 – Happy 50th birthday Enoch (Ian Dunn), a pleasant, chirpy Yorkshire man I met through Sam Excell and Russell Hall. And happy first wedding anniversary to Phil's stepsister Ali and her feller Terry.

I was at the ceremony and reception in Poole with Paula – and to top it off nicely, Paula learned later that day that she'd become a grandma again. So it's happy first birthday Mattea.

On the album front, I've been immersing myself in three sold gold classics – Life's Rich Pageant by REM, Marquee Moon by Television and The Icicle Works' eponymous first LP.

But it's an REM song from a later album that I can't get out of my head at the moment – you know the one, "It's the end of the world as we know it and I feel fine."

Sadly, it would have been just as appropriate had war-minded Hillary Clinton got in.

November 11 – Armistice Day, when millions stop what they're doing, stay quiet and say nothing for two minutes at 11am to honour and respect the fallen and maimed in all conflicts since World War One, which ended on the 11th hour of the 11th day of the 11th month in 1918.

Canadian singer songwriter Leonard Cohen has passed away aged 82. Often criticized and parodied for his so-called depressing, wrist-slashing music, he was actually a great poet and songwriter with insight, passion, humour, sensitivity and poise – a class act loved by millions.

Street violence has erupted across the USA following Donald Trump's election. He's seen as a divisive force set to tear the country apart. But the Republican president-elect's response has been that at least the riots show citizens have passion for a country he's trying to unite.

His defeat of Democrat rival Hillary Clinton is seen in some quarters as a huge shock, just like Britain's referendum result, where a majority voted for us to leave the European Union.

Sure, I was surprised at both – I thought we'd narrowly plump to stay in the EU and Clinton would just scrape into the White House by an equally narrow margin. But big shocks? – Nah!

I think each is a strong indicator of something that's becoming more apparent by the week – namely, that people are so sick to the back teeth of a corrupt political establishment they no longer trust and are starting to actually hate that they're searching desperately for alternatives.

Or at least, what are being presented as alternatives. In Trump's case the disillusioned have possibly been seriously misled – we'll have to see. His election could well prove a disaster for America and us all. But I maintain that so could Hillary's have been – maybe more so.

For starters, she's part of a powerful alliance squaring up to Russia in a hazardous tit-for-tat flexing of military muscles. Apparently, Clinton and Putin hate and distrust each other but he's gone on record saying he could work with Donald to their countries' mutual benefit.

And Clinton is just as controversial as Trump – she with her allegedly very dark and dodgy activities and he with his supposedly insensitive, intolerant and inflammatory comments.

Turning to the EU referendum, I feel many people – me included – saw it as a chance to register disgust at the capitulation of our countries to the oppressive and intrusive machinery of a super state that's been steadily eroding democracy, national sovereignty and identity.

In short, our referendum and Trump's victory both evidenced a sincere, heart-felt but maybe misdirected bid to claim back our lands from an uncaring and exploitative ruling network.

Elsewhere in today's news, the UN asserts that Islamic State has killed dozens of civilians as perceived traitors as fighting rages on between rival factions in Mosul city, Iraq.

And six men and a woman died and more than 50 people were injured when a tram derailed and crashed in Croydon, London.

November 12 – Like many lads of my age growing up, I was a huge fan of the *Man from UNCLE* spy adventure TV series and movies starring Robert Vaughn and David McCallum.

So it's with sadness I hear of the passing of Vaughn, aged 83. He had leukaemia.

The American actor also featured in various other hit TV shows and blockbuster films. I loved him in the stylish Hustle TV series and he was also briefly in Coronation Street.

In the footballing world, England's national team stays top of its World Cup qualifying group thanks to a 3-0 drubbing of old rivals Scotland last night.

Yesterday – as usual for a Friday – I had drinks and laughs at Sam's with her, Carl, Tina and Jem, and later today I'm off to the Bell for a charity day in aid of Macmillan Cancer Support.

November 12, 10pm – The Macmillan fundraiser was a damp squib – heavy rain and a general lack of interest meant it was scrapped, which I discovered on sauntering up to the pub this afternoon.

But it turned out to be an okay couple of hours – Nicola, Laura, Mikey Vicky Brown, Mark Thornton, Ben Avill, Ian "Longshanks", old boy Joe and others were there to talk to. Cool!

I had three pints, went home for a few hours and returned this evening, to find the bar populated by Tony Jeffery, Lottie Wragg, Matt Brant, Ollie Okoye, Tim Robbins, John Gaynor, Lou Delahaye, Brian, Jim, Mark and Laura and adorable pub puppy Flick.

Plus my long-time pal Pete Rowsen – one of the "Devon seven" from *Volume One*.

Afternoon boozing meant I was pretty wiped out on resuming my drinking session. I took ages finishing my first evening pint and then left, feeling I'd had enough. It's an age and health thing you know.

My good pal and Bell bar manager Nicola Williams has just secured a teaching assistant post – first step in a career she's hankered after for ages. She's worked at the pub for six years and her cheery face will be missed behind the bar – though she'll continue to socialize there.

Well done Nic, the pub won't be the same without you on the team. We're all so proud of you, "adopted daughter" – all the best for your new adventure.

To explain, the lovely Nicola is my "daughter number two." My son Phil's wife Emily is number one in the absence of any female blood children.

November 13 – It's Remembrance Sunday, a time to respect and honour the war dead and devastated while cursing the bloody politicians.

For it is they who get us into conflicts, expect decent, honourable patriots to fight them, callously cast the damaged survivors aside afterwards and then have the sickening gall to lay poppy wreaths at the Cenotaph on this poignant anniversary. Bastards!

I shall observe the customary two minutes' silence at 11am after a trip to the corner shop. But for now it's a quick check on Facebook and breakfast.

Oh, by the way, it's the first anniversary of the Paris terror attacks that killed 130 and injured hundreds. War and peacetime mass murder, crazed zealots and political nut jobs. Pah!

As if to ram home the point, over 50 people have been killed and more than 100 injured in an alleged suicide bomber's assault on an Islamic shrine in Pakistan following evening prayers.

This is tragically commonplace in a country that's been a hotbed of political conflict and bloody violence for years.

Meanwhile, Nigel Farage has become the first British politician to meet Donald Trump after his election as US president. To see that embarrassing loon cosying up to the new leader of the free world is cringe worthy but I know why Farage went to the States for this meeting.

It's because both men are seen as mavericks successfully challenging the corrupt global political establishment. If only that were true. They're as much part of the gang as anyone – just presented as outsiders to fool the public, large swathes of which have bought the lie.

It's a PR job, pure and simple – manipulation of the masses by giving them the illusion of choice. No-one gets to the position of Trump – or even Farage – without the support of some very powerful and influential people in the very establishment they purport to oppose.

Fake realities, twisted images, smoke and mirrors, deception, chicanery, naked greed and ruthless ambition – This is our screwed-up world, 2016. And that's the way it's been for eons.

November 13, 10.30pm – Just had a very enjoyable Remembrance Sunday hi-jinks session at the Bell with a lot of drunken ex-service folk and others. It was grand!

The former military people included karaoke deejay Ross Maslin (pissed), John Palmer (pissed), Paul Clyde (pissed), karaoke champion Darren Spence (pissed), his lovely wife Sarah (pissed but impressively keeping up) and my good friend Tina McNally (probably pissed but not showing it too much).

Our drinks were being served by Nicola Williams and Tony Jeffery and also there were Billy Clarkson, Kelly Adams, Ruth Troke,

Simon Turnbull, Matt Brant, John Gaynor, Shannon Hanlon, Mark Chastney, Guus Bruin, Brian, Darren and pub runners Laura and Mark. Great!

The new series of I'm a Celebrity Get Me Out of Here started while I was at the pub and it's still on TV as I type.

This year's campmates include Countdown's Carol Vorderman, EastEnders and Gavin and Stacey star Larry Lamb, Emmerdale's Adam Thomas, Scarlett Moffatt of Gogglebox, TV presenter and fashion model Lisa Snowden and ex-footballer Wayne Bridge. Plus, as is increasingly the case nowadays, a bunch of people I've never heard of. I must be getting old!

My personal favourite is Scarlett, who I really like. She's been great in Gogglebox – pleasant, thoughtful and funny – and must be among the front runners to take the crown. But I also like Larry, and part of me feels it's high time an older, more established person won.

In recent years it's been mostly younger contestants grabbing the glory – folk I've not been aware of until they appeared on I'm a Celebrity.

Nothing wrong with that – I love Stacey Solomon thanks to this programme; and Vicky Pattison, Kian Egan and Dougie Poynter were also worthy victors, as was Gino D'Acampo.

I wouldn't mind seeing Adam or Carol doing well and reaching the final. But victory for Larry would place him in the footsteps of Tony Blackburn, Phil Tufnell, Carol Thatcher, Christopher Biggins and Carl Fogarty as a more senior, better known jungle monarch.

Whoever triumphs in the end, I'm looking forward immensely to this latest series of the only so-called reality TV show I'm interested in. For me, the jungle setting makes it different and compelling. I love it – both the ITV One programme and its ITV Two companion.

November 15, 4pm – Just arrived home from the Bell, where I've had a great afternoon in the company of Dave Froud, Nicola

Williams. Mikey Delahaye, Laura Williams, Mark and Harry Evans, old boy Joe, Ian "Longshanks" and others.

Chatting to Dave, I realized I knew his dad from way back. I love it when that happens!

November 16 – Wishing a very happy birthday to my friend Victoria Brown, who's been a firm supporter of my books from the start so qualifies as among the handful of people who automatically get a signed copy of each new one published, free and gratis from yours truly.

It's also Brian Quilter's birthday – Phil's step-brother and his best man when he wed Emily. Not only that, Mark Painter – Cheryl's son, Phil's cousin – is 30. Best wishes to them too.

Spain scored twice late in the game to pull off a 2-2 draw against England's footballers in a televised friendly at Wembley last night – a disappointing end to Gareth Southgate's four-match tenure as interim manager. Now the question is will he or someone else be appointed?

Also on the TV front, I'm once again loving I'm a Celebrity, especially the highly likeable Scarlett Moffatt, the chirpy 26-year-old from County Durham. Larry Lamb's doing well too.

For the record, the other contestants I haven't mentioned yet are Sam Quek, a member of Britain's gold-medal winning female Olympic hockey team, comedian Joel Dommett, Jordan Banjo of dance group Diversity and former Strictly Come Dancing professional Ola Jordan.

Yet to appear in the jungle are two more – TV and radio presenter Danny Baker and Martin Roberts, best known for hosting the telly show Homes Under the Hammer.

Been playing Beatles for Sale, Help! and Revolver. Next it'll be Rubber Soul. Bliss!

Flirting hard with Saturn
Truth reveals a pattern.

November 18 – Today is a sad one. It's Steve Yarwood's funeral, so I'm off to that ruddy crematorium yet again later on, this time to pay my respects to my great pal, buddy and bro.

"Soapbox" Steve is one of the best male friends I've ever made. His jet black humour was a tonic as I faced my terrifying heart crisis. I've lit a candle and written a Facebook tribute.

I've referred to Steve quite a few times in my books, including one mention of a boozy day trip to Poole a couple of years back, after which I referred to us as "two ageing gits growing old disgracefully and not giving a toss." Pretty much summed us up.

Farewell Steve – till we meet again. RIP matey.

Just playing the Beatles' first album Please Please Me – still sounding as fresh, clean, interesting and inspiring as it did when made in 1963. An amazing debut by all accounts.

I've lined up With the Beatles – their second where they showed just how well their song writing skills were coming along – to listen to next.

Then it will be the later long players Yellow Submarine (1999 song track version), Sergeant Pepper, Magical Mystery Tour and Abbey Road, continuing the Fab Four theme. Music at its very best – oh yes!

November 19, 11am – Steve's funeral was a tough ordeal for his family and friends. The decidedly non-religious crematorium service for my atheist chum was attended by his long-time partner Jill, his mum and dad, brother Wayne, sisters Jane and Sarah, daughter Emma, sons Jake and Daryl, Daryl's partner and my friend Clare Hayes, Steve's mates and mine Jem Hannen, Rod Marlow and Mark Hemington, Jill's workmate Lesley and others.

From the "crem" we went on to the Commodore Hotel on Southbourne cliff top, close to Steve's flat, for the wake.

Later on some of us ended up at the Bell, where we met "my daughter" Nicola Williams, John Palmer, Mikey Delahaye, his mum Lou, her feller Brian, Krissie Benbow, Paul Clyde, Alex King, Demi Pitkin, John Gaynor, guv'nor Mark Evans and deejay Ross Maslin.

Seeing all those lovely people and listening to Ross's memory-jogging 1990's set was just what I needed after the sad and heavy afternoon proceedings.

Another spirit-lifting event came earlier today when I met my new friend Sue Seeney and her adorable dogs – seven-year-old brother and sister spaniels Buddy and Poppy – for coffee at a cliff top cafe then by a bracing walk along the prom as we talked about a range of subjects.

I thoroughly enjoyed the company and chat during this exhilarating break from my normal routine on a blue-sky crisp but sunny morning. We're going to do it again three weeks today.

November 20 – Yesterday (Saturday) afternoon was fab too – even though it rained. I went to the pub, which was packed out for Bournemouth's festive carnival and a weekend devoted to world-famous local author Mary Shelley, creator of the classic horror novel *Frankenstein*.

So it was all scary costumes, marching bands and other fancy-dressed revelling. It was also my mate Jeff McNally's birthday and he was there with wife Tina and several other Homes for Heroes fundraisers – the ex-service people's charity jointly benefitting from the frivolity.

The other worthy cause being funded was the People's Dispensary for Sick Animals – PDSA.

I met and spoke to loads of friendly, familiar faces – far too many to list here, but I will name check a select few, such as Jeff's niece Nicole, the talented young singer-songwriter who blew me away at Boscombe Community Fair (see Chapter Seven).

I also ran into my former workmate Patsy and her man Scott, who I hadn't seen to speak to for ages, and Kathy Dickinson, who I met last year at one of Sam and Carl's barbecues.

Dave Froud took along his steam engine – his great passion.

My pal Matt Brant was there with his little daughter Layla, as were Jem, Nicola and a host of other buddies and mates. And I had a long, interesting chin wag with Victoria Brown about friends and families. All in all, it was a smashing day.

November 21 – Had another blast at the Bell last night with Laura and Mark, Jem, Penny, Matt, Johns P and G, Mark H, Alex, Guus, Gemma, Lottie, Jane, Ricky and DJ Ross. Cool!

I've experienced the extremes of life's highs and lows, all in one weekend. It's been an appropriate three-day reflection of my entire year – one of personal joy and sadness and good and bad stuff happening to me and people across the globe.

Our steady slide into World War Three has been accompanied by bloody battles, sickening terrorist attacks and a perturbing shift to the right in political thinking at home and abroad, evidenced by the rise of Nigel Farage and UKIP, the victory of Republican Trump and similar developments in France and elsewhere.

It's time to start bringing this latest instalment of my life journal to a close.

November 22 – But first I must say happy 27th birthday to Phil, my son and my rock.

Dazzled by Miss Conduct
Shown to be the wrong fuck
Sentenced by Judge Mental
Getting strict parental.

Well, that's Halloween and Bonfire night out of the way and I'm a Celebrity back on television, where the adverts are once again getting schmaltzy and soppy. Glittering decorations and plastic trees have started appearing all over the place. Do I hear sleigh bells?

****

CHAPTER TWELVE

Spread The Love

November 23 – It's been a year of mixed fortunes for me, terrible, tragic moments but joyful, encouraging ones too. The passing of Cousin Sandra and my two very close buddies Theresa Bevis and Steve Yarwood were very, very low points. And the couple bit split from Paula.

But I've kept her as a dear pal, made new ones, strengthened ties with some really lovely people, become reunited with long-standing chums and had many good times and laughs.

Certain folk might be puzzled by some of the strange stuff I come up with and my strong desire to put it all out there. But this is what I am. This is what I do. Take it or leave it – I just ask you to understand it.

And so we start the descent into Christmas – our annual tinsel-strewn, booze-soaked Hell fest that paradoxically remains my favourite time of year.

I love the harmonic, unifying goodwill to all men aspect of it – the most important by far but rudely thrust aside far too often quite violently by the more ugly features of the party season.

I detest the two-month garish commercialized run up and the fact that the event itself heightens tensions between people to the point of bitter clashes and massive fall-outs.

I have my own deeply personal reasons to hate this time of year with its fake trees and forced jollity. But I don't – I actually relish it. Always have and sincerely hope I always shall.

I yearn for peace on Earth. Keep spreading that love people. Till next time…

Tatty-bye, M.M.
November 23, 2016

****

173

****

Control a man's property and you control his life, control his dreams and you control his soul.

You don't have to be joined at the hip and tied to a treadmill to have unity of purpose.

Pure instinct tells me that, at the end of the day, it's all going to turn out all right.

Searching for truth is like peeling an onion. Just when you've stripped back one layer of perception, another appears and you feel compelled to keep on going.

Three little words can mask a world of pain and torment, misery and sadness – and they are "yes, I'm fine."

Attitude can be okay – cool even – if backed up by talent or wisdom. But far too often it's just irritating crap.

"War is when your government tells you who the enemy is. A revolution is when you figure it out yourself" – Anonymous.

"Change the way you look at things and things you look at change" – Wayne Dyer.

This book is dedicated to my dear cousin Sandra and my great buddy Steve Yarwood, who both passed away as I was writing it.

And it honours the hugely beneficial influence other have had on my life – Mum, Dad, Jan, Carol and David, Suzette, aunts and uncles. Phil and family, Joe, Paula. Dawn and my amazing friends. Thanks for making it bearable and actually quite fun for much of the time.

Keep smiling, spread the love, make peace with each other and laugh – a lot...

**The spark of Consciousness in this flesh,
blood and bone organism called Martin Money.**

ABOUT THE AUTHOR

Born in Slough on February 25, 1954, Martin Moncy lived there until early adulthood, moving to Dorset in 1978.

Leaving school with three A Levels and seven O Levels, he worked in a bank for a few months before starting a 24-year career in regional journalism that ended in redundancy in 1997.

Since then he's had a variety of part-time jobs and also worked as a volunteer for charities.

A proud father and grandfather, he lives in Bournemouth where he enjoys short cliff-top walks, writing, reading, listening to music, watching TV and socialising.

Author's photo by Sam Excell

9 781787 192010